Arriving Here: Reflections from the Hearth and Trail

In the powerful tradition of Annie Dillard, John Muir, and Rachel Carson, yet with her own unique lyricism, Lisa offers us a precious and wise handbook of both companionship and connection.... While this dear book is a treat to read at any time of year, it may be best to slow your reading down, to read only Lisa's words that describe the current season, so specifically precious are her words of wisdom and companionship. Yet it does us immediate good to mouth and inhale her closing verse, "Consider the Raindrop."

—Jacob Watson, author of *Essence: The Emotional Path to Spirit* and *Enso Morning: Daily Meditation Gifts*

Arriving Here *offers us a sensitive and insightful look into the micro and macro, the momentary and the timeless, the personal and the universal, all at the same time. Adopting an ageless pattern as a lens to make sense of her life, Lisa makes the subtle explicit and the mundane sacred.... This book will warm hearts, ground us in gratitude, and raise our sense of responsibility.*

—Robert Atkinson, PhD, author of *Mystic Journey* and *The Story of Our Time*

Being human is to live out variations on a theme, or a collection of themes.... We seek to craft, from the twinkles of insight along the way, a coherent constellation of purpose. That's what Lisa Steele-Maley has accomplished in Arriving Here. *And in sharing her reflections, Lisa invites each of her readers to gaze back, gaze up, gaze all around, and do the same.*

—Aram Mitchell, Executive Director of Renewal in the Wilderness

Arriving Here

Reflections from the Hearth and Trail

Lisa Steele-Maley

LAMPYRIDAE, LLC

Arriving Here: Reflections from the Hearth and Trail
2020 © Lisa Steele-Maley
ISBN 978-1-7361453-0-2

Cover Photograph: Lisa Steele-Maley
Developmental Editor and Proofreader: Laura Case Larson
Copy Editor and Proofreader: Amy Stackhouse
Book and Cover Designer: Lindy Gifford
Publisher: Lampyridae, LLC

In service to a life of connection

&

with gratitude for my family ~ past, present, and future

Preface

This is the story of finding the purpose in my life and living into that purpose more deeply. As my story, it may hold no particular significance to anyone but me. However, we can learn a lot by hearing one another's stories. Our individual experiences of living in this world are not really singular. We are all connected. And so I share this particular story as encouragement to those who are seeking meaning in their lives in this time and place. May it serve you, and together may we serve the greater cause of life's longing for itself. May we live toward our eternal purpose in each daily, mundane action. In so doing, may our awareness light the way toward an earthly life that honors our interdependent reality.

The author and activist Joanna Macy has identified that we, as a society, have arrived at a threshold. In *Active Hope: How to Face the Mess We're in without Going Crazy*, Macy and Chris John-stone offer two perspectives from which we can view our current situation: we can recognize the current time and place as the "Great Unraveling," or we can recognize it as the "Great Turning." I have found myself, as an individual, at this threshold.

The Great Unraveling recognizes that the world as we know it is collapsing. Economic, political, social, and ecological systems are irreparably broken. Enough pieces have fallen out of the structure that the collapse is taking on a life of its own. The rule of the patriarchy is ending, and the -isms that have kept it in place for centuries are going with it. We cannot yet see what will replace it. There is an uncertainty inherent in the Great Unraveling. Something is being dismantled, and the replacement has not yet arrived.

The Great Turning, on the other hand, describes our individual and collective turning away from destructive, consumptive ways of being and toward a life-sustaining society. As our frame of reference shifts, our relationships with one another and with the earth shift too. Our commitment to think and act on behalf of all life on Earth supports and is supported by our species' evolution of consciousness. The Great Turning brings us back into a right relationship with the living world—into belonging, participation, and interconnection.

Ideally, we live our lives with awareness and action in a way that honors the truth of both: the world as we know it is unraveling *and* human consciousness is turning. They go hand in hand. I can see how this is true in my daily life. My world is unraveling and my consciousness is evolving as I release old stories of individualism and separation and step into connection and oneness. This is a spiritual shift, affecting the way I think and feel about myself, the world, and my place in it. It is also a practical shift, affecting the way in which I live my days and nights. The two, the spiritual and the physical, have proved themselves to be inseparable, woven together by my own emotional responses and intellectual curiosity.

As I have stepped toward my own turning, I have felt my life energy for supporting the Great Turning increase. As my connection to the land and my community deepens, I feel increasing resolve to support our wholeness. Sharing my evolution in this story, at this time, is an offering to our collective turning.

May something in my story support your evolving story.

May my sense of purpose enliven your sense of purpose.

May my strategies of connection help you find your own strategies of connection.

May your emerging story bring purpose and clarity to your days.

May your life provide inspiration for someone else's.

Contents

Introduction

My first book, *Without a Map: A Caregiver's Journey through the Wilderness of Heart and Mind*, describes the years I spent supporting my dad as dementia interrupted his life and then as he died, and relates them to other personal experiences, namely living in the wilderness and parenting. On the eve of the book's publication, I suddenly began to wonder if there was more to the story. I wondered if exploring more of my life, including those aspects that seemed unrelated, would help me find a clearer path forward from the present moment. I sensed that, through deeper exploration of my life's story, I might be able to uncover a bigger picture, one that might point me toward my soul's purpose and provide greater insight into how I could more effectively do the work that I am meant to be doing in this lifetime.

What if I considered the caregiving years within the context of my entire life's journey, not just the years of living and working in the natural world?

What if I explored the bits of insight that each story could give me about myself and my place within the order of the universe?

What if I identified and named the brushes with grace that have found me throughout my life?

Introduction

In this time of searching, I stumbled upon a quote from the writer Florida Scott-Maxwell's *The Measure of My Days*: "You need only claim the events of your life to make yourself yours. When you truly possess all you have seen and done ... you are fierce with reality."

I was ready and eager to become fierce with reality.

When I met Robert Atkinson, a Maine-based teacher and author who has developed a framework for personal mythmaking, I began to see a manageable way into my work. Bob was generous with his time and encouragement, and I began to explore my life story using the framework he describes in *The Gift of Stories: Practical and Spiritual Applications of Autobiography, Life Stories, and Personal Mythmaking*. Bob introduced me to the hero's journey, articulated by Joseph Campbell, as a way of exploring personal life history in a universal context. The hero's journey describes the process of stepping away from the inherited life of our culture, encountering challenges, finding allies, struggling, resting, and eventually meeting a final challenge that solidifies the learning that we required from our journey. With the journey complete, we travel home to share what we have learned. The hero's journey is articulated through any one of a number of triads: separation, initiation, return; beginning, conflict, resolution; birth, death, rebirth; wrestle, rest, return. As Bob describes it, this sacred pattern can play out in our lives internally or externally. Identifying the mythic pattern in our lives invites us out of our individual journeys and into the universal human story. We are all heroes on a journey.

I became convinced that finding a common thread in my own life would reveal a thread that extended into the eternal. With trepidation and anticipation, I began the process of inquiry and self-study required to understand my own hero's journey. As I began, Bob offered a bit of advice that I took as a word of caution: while I would learn a lot as I remembered and reclaimed the journey of the past, the most important aspect of my mythmaking exercise would be what I would *do* with what I *learned*.

"A Call to Adventure: Seeking" is the retrospective that emerged from reviewing my life experiences using the mythic journey framework. Using the framework as a guide to remembering my own life circumstances, I found a continuity and clarity of purpose that I had not previously seen on my life path. I recognized repeating patterns of wrestle and rest, and I recalled glimpses of the divine, infinite, and eternal that had punctuated my mundane life periodically. Those moments appeared out of nowhere and then, just as quickly, faded back into the ordinary without language, context, and a system of beliefs to ground them. Recalling these glimpses into the sacred, I recognized that they, in fact, were the path to the clarity that I had been seeking. As the poet William Stafford describes in "The Way It Is,"

> There's a thread you follow. It goes among
> things that change. But it doesn't change.
> People wonder about what you are pursuing.
> You have to explain about the thread.
> But it is hard for others to see.
> While you hold it you can't get lost.

By the time I finished my life review, I was holding the elusive thread in my hand. I discovered that my soul wishes only to remain in union with the universal consciousness of which we are all a part. It is embodied in this form in this time and place for only a short while. As long as it is here, it wishes to bridge the chasms that separate and isolate us in this lifetime and reclaim the unity of all creation. Throughout my life, I have seen glimpses and heard the voices of this truth, but I wasn't always paying attention. I am paying attention now, and I notice that I am continually invited to participate in the flow of life that surrounds me. I just need to continue to step into it, expressing and celebrating oneness with the human family, the earth, and the Universal Spirit.

Introduction

"A Call to Wholeness: Remembering" and "A Call to Action: Deepening" contain reflections from the two years since my initial return from that mythic journey. Using the seasons of the year as an anchor, I recognize anew my belonging to the wider world. My body, heart, and mind fall into rhythm with the world around me, remembering that I am always a part of it, never apart from it. As I move forward with what I have learned, my eyes are open to the mystery and beauty around me in a new way. Not only am I recognizing the sacred in the everyday, I am paying close attention to its presence everywhere and in everyone. I am reclaiming my vibrant participation in the web of creation and settling more deeply into my sense of belonging and responsibility.

I could not have arrived here by looking outward to any expert, teacher, or belief system. I could only arrive more fully at the ground beneath my feet after a deep inward search that spanned miles and decades.

A Call to Adventure
Seeking

Awakening to Awe

Rising Sun
Waning moon
In me, of me
Over, under, around, through
World soul
Listening
Attending
Presenting
In me, of me
Beautiful Mystery

Separation

The separation phase of the mythic pattern involves a departure from one place to another, or an inner separation that leads from one status to another. In either case, it begins with a "Call to Adventure" that signals the beginning of a new life.

—Robert Atkinson, *The Gift of Stories*

Like many young adults, when I launched into adulthood I was seeking something that couldn't be found in childhood—independence, exploration, and participation in a world of deep meaning and importance to someone other than myself or my family. I wanted to find *my* place in the world. Somehow, the life I had been born into no longer seemed to be the life I was meant to live. There was a vague sense of disconnect, which I associated with being in the wrong time and place or with the wrong people, or with satisfying the wrong purpose. The upwardly mobile world around me felt too fast, too impersonal, and too focused on a future that was always just beyond my reach. The pace and priorities didn't match with the sensibility and sensitivity that were trying to blossom within me. I didn't know what the right place or purpose would look like, but I thought I would know it when I found it. Eventually, my search for belonging led me to the wilderness.

There, I felt held by a largesse that embraced and began to melt my wondering, wandering, worrying ways. In their place, I gained courage, perception, and strength. My internal world began to respond to the rhythms of the natural world, and I felt at home in myself in a way I hadn't before. The natural world held a mystery that I could live with. I didn't need to know everything; I just knew I was home. I felt known and connected to something outside of myself in a way that felt both new and exciting and ancient and familiar. I was filled with a sense of belonging and purpose in the work I did for and with the earth. In my first summer off the beaten path, I worked on a trail crew in southeast Alaska.

One summer afternoon, I walked up the trail and lost myself. Under the wide sky and with my feet firmly on the ground, a fog rolled in. It was so thick I nearly merged with it. I could no longer see two feet in front of my face, but I trusted the ground beneath my feet and I knew my purpose. I was scratching a trail into a scree field, an attempt to keep hikers on the path where they would do less damage to the fragile glacial moraine and be less likely to wander to its dangerous edges. My purpose was singular, and my movements felt both suspended and supported by the icy, enveloping fog. Continual motion was the best way to make a meaningful impact on this hard and unrelenting piece of earth, and it was the only way to stay warm.

Out of the fog, my grandfather's voice came to me, strong and clear. I heard poignant words I remembered him saying to me years ago: "I am so proud of you." I was surprised, comforted, and also certain that I had really heard these words, that they had cut through the fog despite the fact that he had died a month earlier, several hundred miles away. None of my crew members were around, so I couldn't have been hearing their voices. I had heard my grandfather's voice. I worried that hypothermia might be setting in and wondered if I should stop work and get back to camp.

Before I could turn wondering into decision, the sun pierced the fog and warmed me from the outside, with the resonance of my grandfather's voice warming me from the inside. I put down my Pulaski, took off my hood, and turned my face to meet the sun, absorbing its warmth and trying to take in the words I had heard.

I had been touched by something my heart and mind did not have the capacity to grasp. I was grateful for the validation and appreciation. It felt just like my grandfather and also like more than him. Nothing in my life had prepared me to fully appreciate the knowing and love that transcend both life and death, or the universal that can be expressed in the personal. With the echo of my grandfather's voice penetrating the thick fog and unrelenting trail, I became aware of my singular sense of purpose and belonging to that moment. The familiar words offered a sense of connection to an unfamiliar wholeness and assured me that here, with my mind, body, and heart working in concert for something beyond myself, I was on the right path.

Assistance

)

In our new realm, we soon recognize that we are never alone. We always seem to encounter a protective figure, someone or something that is in the right place at the right time, to help us through an impasse. In traditional literature, this aid usually comes in the form of a supernatural helper, a power animal, or a wise elder. In all cases, the assistance brings with it the sensation and assurance that we are being guided.

—Robert Atkinson, *The Gift of Stories*

In Alaska, elements of the natural world—especially the trees, salmon, and eagles—nudged me into living more deeply with the earth's cycles and my own self-awareness. The towering trees offered protection, nurturance, and a reminder to be humble. The salmon who swam the waters, returning to their home rivers to spawn, showed me a life guided by clear inner knowing and a pursuit of basic mandates: get to the ocean, survive, eat, return to the river, spawn, die. Some species return to freshwater to spawn for several years in a row, others return only once before dying; they navigate using cues from the earth's magnetic field and olfactory memory—the imprint of smell. I was envious of their straightforward discipline, their simple trajectory. To my respect for the salmon's simplicity, I hinged an appreciation for the eagle's devotion. Eagles mate for life, returning to the same nest year after year to raise their young. Their connection to each other and to their home territory supported my simmering desire to grow roots, to find rest in a place, and to find companionship.

I met my future husband, Thomas, around this time. We were in love from our first hug, when his joy, courage, and warmth swept me off my feet. The twinkle in his eyes and spring in his step communicated that he was a person of this land, a creature of the same wild space that had opened my heart and welcomed me into its wholeness. He says that it was my smell—the smell of a five-day drive up the Alcan (a.k.a. the Alaska Highway)—that attracted him to me. That's love! I realized quickly that I didn't know what to do with the overwhelming love and enthusiasm I felt. I had to learn how to trust, how to be open, how to be vulnerable, and how to be a good partner. Thomas was patient and learning relationship lessons of his own. The land held us both with wide arms as we walked each other through the joys and challenges that arose as we began to build a life together.

We had grown accustomed to walking away from our cabin and the road that led to it, moving instead toward the river when we wanted to explore. Along the river, we followed the tracks of the critters that had passed before us and explored the banks on both sides. The river led to a neighbor's house, where we frequently visited and sometimes did odd jobs. Beyond that, it led deep into the Takshanuk Mountains. More often than not, we walked and explored without a destination or objective. The expansiveness around us seemed to have carved out an expansiveness within us.

One sunny winter morning, we walked in a less familiar direction, toward the intersection of the dirt road that led to our cabin and the two-lane highway that wound twenty-five miles into town. We wanted to visit the trees we had named the Grove of the Patriarchs, a tall band of elder trees that felt comforting and nourishing. I don't remember the exact circumstances, but I suspect we had gone to them for sustenance and renewal. Their acidic needles fell to the ground regularly to keep the forest floor barren, and their thick canopy caught most of the snow. It was late winter, and the forest felt more open than usual. We had passed the darkest days of winter, and the sun was getting higher and brighter by the day. With the thick understory of devil's club and highbush cranberry suppressed by snow, we could see between and beyond the mature trunks of the trees. Standing under the protective branches of the high trees, we scanned to pick our direction of travel from the grove. We were drawn to a cluster of low spruce trees a few hundred yards away. They seemed to be glowing. Pushing through the tight cluster of young trees, we found ourselves suddenly in a magical winter fairyland. There was a frozen pond in the center of the ring of trees, and there were ice crystals everywhere. They hung on every inward-facing branch of every tree, stood upright atop the icy surface of the pond, and were suspended in the top layer of ice on the pond. In the sparkling stillness there was a feeling of immense joy. We erupted in giggles of delight and words of wonder and surprise.

Our curious minds wanted to know how it had happened. Had the water been open recently? Was it a spring? How many of these young trees would be able to grow to maturity in this small space? Were there conditions beyond this water source that had created such abundant growth? Was the joy we felt emanating from the trees? Did they delight in their habitat as much as we did? But none of the answers, or even the questions, really mattered.

The spruce nursery was as close to magical as I could imagine. I was mesmerized by the resilient young trees, the frozen ice crystals, and the intricate patterns that they had made on every available surface and even within the layers of ice. Awestruck, I knelt on my knees, gazing into the ice. Drawn deeply into the relationship between the trees, water, sun, and cold, I suddenly knew myself as a member of that community. We were beautiful, complex, singular, and intimately connected in this same mysterious life. I stayed there, welcomed and stunned, until the cold crept into my knees, hands, and feet.

As we turned to leave, we thanked the spruce nursery for the joy and peace that it had invited us into. We pledged to return often, though I don't think we ever did. Our habit of moving toward open spaces, new territory, and fresh possibilities continued to guide our days.

Initial Challenge

Contemporary versions of this motif, of crossing the first threshold, would include any experience that gives us a new level of challenges to deal with, such as beginning graduate work, raising children for the first time, a promotion, more responsibilities, doing something new for the first time, struggles in a marriage, and fears of what lies ahead. This motif means we need to summon our courage and advance toward the danger anyway.

—Robert Atkinson, *The Gift of Stories*

After a few years of living deeply in the natural world but quite removed from the human world, Thomas and I began to wonder what was next. We both knew that we were meant to make a contribution to the wider world. Being full of love and joy and offering our gifts to the earth was not a sufficient response to the urge to contribute and participate that we both felt. We didn't yet know *what* we were supposed to be doing or even *how* to begin to figure it out. But we did know that we wanted to have children. That seemed like a reasonable place to begin to figure it all out.

When I got pregnant, we began to seriously consider the logistics of pregnancy and parenting in our remote cabin in the Alaskan woods. We gathered information and advice from books that addressed pregnancy and childbirth as medical processes. The medical clinic in town would offer prenatal care, but it did not support births. To have a medically supervised birth, we would have to incur the expense and travel to get to Juneau or to Whitehorse in the Yukon Territory—both five hours away when the weather was good. We had a few friends and neighbors whom we could rely on at any time of day or night. Living remotely, we were accustomed to borrowing flour from one another, discussing bear activity in our "yards," and sharing care for dogs, houses, cabins, and trails when people were away. They were good company, but we had not formed strong bonds. We didn't feel like we had a strong *community*. This hadn't mattered while we were getting to know one another, focused on deepening our relationship and our connection to the land. But now that we were stepping into uncharted territory, we felt the need for more familiar reassurance and guidance. We wanted an easily available medical community—"just in case"—and, more importantly, we wanted loved ones, friends, and mentors to be nearby. After being immersed in one another and in the forest and river community for several years, it was time to reconnect with the human family.

We moved to Seattle, a city I had lived in and loved years before. My aunt, uncle, cousins, and grandmother lived there and would be a reliable and loving source of comfort and company. We imagined that employment opportunities would be abundant in a big city. We thought of ourselves as capable individuals, ready and willing to do whatever we needed to do to make the transition work. We packed up and moved, prepared to stay with my aunt and uncle for a few days while we found jobs and a place to live.

Within a week, we found an apartment and Thomas found work with a small construction company, but adjusting to the city was tough. We missed being outside, and we missed being together 24/7. Additionally, I found that adjusting to growing a life inside of me was really hard work. I needed to sleep a lot. We would wake early to have breakfast together before Thomas left for his job site. After he left, I would take a nap on the couch, waking midmorning to run or walk along the lakefront a few blocks away. Eventually, I found part-time work on a conservation initiative at a city park where I had worked years before. After hauling our drinking water from nearby springs for several years, we were reminded that we were strangers in a strange land every time we peed into a toilet bowl full of fresh potable water. The rhythm of our days became governed by the financial pressures of urban living rather than the larger seasonal cycles with which we had been so closely aligned. Very quickly, we learned how to balance our well-being, income, sense of purpose, and alignment with values by distributing them between us. As long as we covered all four bases between us, we each felt satisfied we were doing our part.

But this "balance" was tenuous. With so much transition and so much uncertainty ahead of us, we were always on edge. When the water stain on the ceiling in the living room began to bulge, it was a fitting warning sign: the worn and dirty world was leaning in on us. One rainy afternoon, the ceiling literally collapsed, and plaster dust, soggy insulation, and who knows what else landed in our laps. We knew we needed to move and move quickly. After an efficient and focused search, we left a resentful and neglectful landlord and our security deposit behind and moved across town.

With the help of a family member and a hefty mortgage, we bought a small house in a modest family neighborhood. The house was ours, and if the roof fell in we would fix it. This was an incredible reassurance amid the uncertainty of preparing to welcome our son, who was due any day. I attempted to inspire labor contractions by walking the hilly neighborhood every morning and late every afternoon. I met a lot of friendly neighbors who stopped me for pleasant conversation. I think they were often just trying to slow me down so they wouldn't have to assist if my overgrown body suddenly decided it was time to burst. With both my body and our circumstances teetering at the edge of the unknown, life felt overwhelming. Being in motion offered comfort and the illusion that I was in control of something. Additionally, the expanses of the sky and Puget Sound were capacious enough to hold all of my discomfort and invite solace.

After Duncan was born, he and I continued to walk together, only now he was on the outside. As he grew bigger, he moved from a front pack to a stroller and I began to run again. My favorite run took us down the hill from our house, along a beachside trail through a park, and up the hill into the forest above the park. As my body recovered after pregnancy, I also recovered a connection to the environment around me. We were nourished by the moist maritime air that hung among the towering Douglas firs and twisted, peeling madrone trees. We ran through the neighborhoods and parks in sunshine and rain. The stroller became a perch from which Duncan could experience the gifts of the world. He often sat with his eyes wide open, seeming to take it all in. Other times, I would look down to find him lulled to sleep by the fresh air and movement. When I became pregnant again, we returned to walking; after Thatcher was born, we upgraded to a double stroller.

One afternoon, when Thatcher was just a few months old and Duncan was just over two, we walked down to the sound. We were all a bit tired and cranky, so we stopped at the little beach just outside of the big park. It was warm and muggy, but it felt good to be out of the house.

I helped Duncan out of the stroller, and he walked straight to the water's edge. We often looked for crabs under the rocks near the water together. Exhausted, I lifted Thatcher out and sat down in the sand at the top of the beach to nurse him. Duncan began throwing rocks. He wasn't just tossing rocks into the sound haphazardly. He threw each one with as much force as he could gather, his little body lurching forward with each throw. Time seemed to stop as he threw rock after rock after rock. We were there for a long time, encircled in the energy of his deep intention to his work. When he was done, he sat down next to me. He looked relieved.

"Wow," I said. "What was that all about?"

"My turg-ey," he replied immediately.

I was stumped. "Can you say that again? I don't understand," I admitted.

"My turg-ey," he repeated, exasperated. How could I not understand? This was clearly so important. I asked him to try to tell me one more time.

"My lopelation," he explained. Oh, of course.

The operation, a day surgery at the local children's hospital, had been a standard procedure in the eyes of the doctor. When we arrived with our hungry and thirsty toddler who would soon be under anesthesia, we quickly realized how complicated people's lives can be. We noticed one young patient who was clearly a regular. She was smiling bravely and greeting the nurses with ease and familiarity while an adult nearby, her mother, I presumed, looked exhausted and worried.

The operation was not standard for our two-year-old. Several days later, the effects of the anesthesia and pain medication were still fading away and Duncan was in periodic pain. Since his language skills were still developing, reasoning and explanation could go only so far. Unable to offer physical comfort, Thomas and I gave what we could—our loving presence and reassurance that it would get better. But it was distressing to face the reality that we would not always be able to ensure comfort for our children. If that was true, the same could surely be said for safety, health, and happiness too.

Clearly we had underestimated how much Duncan understood. We had also underestimated the wisdom that comes from beyond understanding. In those moments on the beach, Duncan had bypassed the realms of knowing and understanding to access his own healing potential. For that moment, I was released from the weight of responsibility that I felt for those two dear, innocent lives, my sons born into this challenging world. In that moment, I was gifted with a lasting reminder that children are, as Kahlil Gibran describes in *The Prophet*, "the sons and the daughters of life's longing for itself." I was assured that the life source from which they came would sustain them.

In those long moments throwing rocks, as Duncan was releasing his unnameable stress and frustration to begin healing the physical and emotional hurts of the operation, all of my parenting anxiety was tossed into the waves, too. No matter what challenges life would throw us, there was something greater that would hold us all and guide us toward whatever we needed. As we sat together looking out over Puget Sound, I rested in the relief that had been offered by the sunny afternoon, the beach full of rocks, and the reassurance of the knowing and nurturing that come from deep within us and beyond us.

Retreat

There comes a time when we need to step back, reconsider things, take care of ourselves, and make our own final preparations for the next threshold that lies ahead of us. It can be a conscious or unconscious withdrawal, but it is a time to reassess where we are and where we may be going, and to do the serious work of looking inward, which ultimately aids our renewal.

—Robert Atkinson, *The Gift of Stories*

When our boys approached school age, we moved across the country. We had grown to love Seattle, had a decent work-life balance, and were making ends meet. We just did not want to continue to raise our boys in the city. We all needed more room to roam. Our hearts yearned for the mountains, but we also wanted community.

As we studied the map in search of the place that would be home, we were drawn to the East Coast. During visits back to my childhood home in Connecticut, we had appreciated the ways in which homes and entire communities were nestled into forests, with lakes and rivers dotting and dashing the landscape. Ecological history and human history seemed to commingle. Not wanting to fall into the fast-paced eastern lifestyle that I had moved away from, we looked to more rural states. Eventually, we decided on Maine. We hoped that the spaciousness and creative, resourceful community that we longed for could be found in the long and winding contours of Maine's coastline.

When we moved, our ideal vision seemed elusive. We started out in a small apartment in a family housing complex just off campus from the university where Thomas was completing a condensed master's program. My attention to the outside world narrowed as my primary focus became juggling each family member's needs, all of us straining to find balance in our new surroundings and responsibilities. We lived just off the bike path that linked the university to two neighboring towns. The family housing complex made it easy to meet people and the boys quickly found playmates. But there was tension in being surrounded by people who, like us, were struggling to make ends meet and get through this stage so they could get on with their lives. As fall turned to winter, the wider world around us became peripheral, and I began to fall into bouts of fatigue, illness, and achy joints and muscles. I never connected one cycle to another and shrugged them off as inconveniences. I remember being so tired trying to play with the boys in the afternoon that I would offer them a choice. Either we could go outside or I would need to take a nap. They usually preferred to go outside, so I rarely took a nap, and I felt like a mess. In addition to being exhausted, I was disappointed in myself. I wasn't parenting the way I wanted to; I wanted to be more available to enjoy and participate in my sons' creative, energetic toddler energy.

When Thomas finished his program, we moved to a rural community with a small elementary school and a good local food co-op. Our new home, an old farmhouse on a big patch of land, needed a lot of work; we spent six months tearing out walls and drop ceilings, converting the attic into living space, and putting in windows—lots of windows. The back of the house opened onto an expansive field rimmed by hardwood forest. A drainage ditch that ran through the field became a creek when it dropped into the woods. Between the house, the field, and the forest, it seemed we had found a lifetime of exploring, discovery, and projects. As Thomas and I settled into work and the boys settled into school, we all began to build connections in the community.

But I was still not myself; I struggled against exhaustion regularly. If I worked or played too much one day, I would need to go slowly and rest the next day. For long periods, I accepted the symptoms as a by-product of growing older, or the stress of adapting to change, or the demands of parenting young children. Other times, I visited the doctor, explained the latest set of symptoms, and hoped for help. After multiple x-rays, a CAT scan, months of physical therapy, and a scary episode of tingling and weakness on one side of my body, I decided to try another medical route. After one visit and a blood test, a naturopathic doctor diagnosed Lyme disease. All of the symptoms that I had alternately shrugged off and battled for several years could be traced back to a tick bite I didn't even remember getting.

Once I had a diagnosis, my attention shifted. I no longer resented my fatigue, but gave into it wholeheartedly. The protocols that my doctor used to treat the Lyme made things worse before they got better. Acknowledging my compromised health and limited capacity meant adding it to the list of things that Thomas and I would need to balance. My retreat into myself in order to recover helped me clarify just how devoted I was to my children and my husband. I measured my energy carefully, knowing that I was allotted only so much each day. I couldn't spend the afternoon baking bread if I wanted to read to the boys at bedtime. I couldn't play hide-and-seek after school if I was in charge of cooking dinner that night. I was also working part-time. Two nights a week, I arrived home from work after the boys had gone to bed. I remember sitting and looking at a plate of spaghetti that Thomas had kept warm for me, overwhelmed by my gratitude for his kindness and the reality that I just couldn't find the energy to eat it.

Slowly, my energy returned. I began to experiment with little bits of exercise to see if it could expand my energy rather than deplete it. Taking short walks in the woods with the boys was a perfect place to start. Picking our way carefully over sticks and rocks and looking around at the season's treasures meant we went slowly and rarely very far. I began to feel like myself again. As I emerged from my narrow Lyme world, I didn't immediately look beyond the walls of our nuclear family. Thomas and the boys had been by my side all along. Settling more deeply into the meaning in my relationships with them, I ceased to sense my need to participate in the larger world. My perspective had constricted, but my yearning to be in connection was as strong as ever.

Dear Mimom,

This morning, I dreamt that we went to the lake for a swim. In the lake, the water held you gently and you moved through it with tender grace and slow strength. The strings that held you to the earth and to me disintegrated. You were deeply trusting of some unfolding process and were clearly both giving in and gathering force. I felt your life force—real, strong, and peaceful as you floated. And I stood on the shore, knowing that while your body was floating toward the willow tree, your spirit was diffusing into the water, into the air, and into me. As the lake gently welcomed your physical body, I watched you go and felt you arrive.

Dabe asks, "Who wants to take Mimom for a swim?" As the grandchildren race eagerly to the lake, I wait while Dabe helps Mimom from her bed and into her bathing suit and waterproof arm cast. When they get downstairs, Mimom and I join arms to continue on to the lake together. As we get closer, she stands more firmly— taller, younger. We slip into the water by the shore, and I watch her motions transform into smooth, fluid, relaxed peace. I encourage her to come up for air and try to untangle her from the ribbons that wrap themselves around her legs and the pier. She blows kisses to me and into the water. Each motion is joyful, peaceful—or maybe each motion is simply a joyful, peaceful release from life, a bridge of the continuum that links life and death. Her spirit is rich, vibrant, and vital, yet she doesn't need to come up for air and doesn't need to be fully untangled from the ribbons in order to swim through the lake that has sustained her family for generations.

I woke from this dream with calm fullness, full of love for the grandmother I knew as Mimom and full of understanding of the love and largesse she embodied. It had been a few years since she had been able to get down the steep steps to the lake, and it was just a few weeks before she died when I described the dream to her in a letter.

Initiation

)

The initiation phase signals an intense period of "Greater Challenges." Here, we meet with various tests and difficult tasks all in succession ... inner struggles where we are forced to face all that lies within us, and to come to know the internal landscape of our psyche more than we had before. This is the heart of the transformation process.

—Robert Atkinson, *The Gift of Stories*

When my dad first began to show signs of needing some support, I didn't think too much of it. I began visiting him more and slowly observed how his needs for care and external support were increasing. As he became more confused, I became more involved, until suddenly we were on the cusp of what would be a four-year period of transition. The narrow lens that I had trained on my nuclear family did not expand much, but it expanded enough to include one more person. Dad began to occupy a lot of my time and attention as I worried about him and learned how best to support him at every new stage. As we accumulated shared experiences, we dug a deep well of love and trust. This well became a source of strength for me. Though he could never tell me, I believe that it was also a source of comfort for Dad as dementia turned his life into an impossible obstacle course.

As I settled in to be both companion and caregiver for Dad, Thomas and the boys lent their full encouragement, freeing me from the guilt and pressure that had originally accompanied spending so much time away from our family. I felt compelled to offer my time and attention, and I was grateful that my family understood that my drive to be in support was more than just a desire. It felt like a responsibility I needed to step into—simply the right thing to do. They responded with abundant concern and love for me as well as a new capacity to care for themselves and each other in ways they had not yet had the need or opportunity to experience.

Early on, I had to teach myself that I could not talk myself out of this work. I was the one to do it. I also hoped for external support, for a map that would come from some "expert" or outside source. There was some guidance here and there, but the only real authorities Dad and I would find were ourselves. When I settled into the wisdom that could only be gleaned from paying attention to and being fully present with one another, there was more than enough information to guide our decisions. Over four years of caregiving, our relationship felt very reciprocal. Dad never had the benefit of knowing how much those years meant to me, but I hope he could feel my gratitude in the time we spent together. Dad's decline with dementia was a tremendous learning experience. For the most part, I couldn't see it at the time. I was just showing up, doing what needed to be done. I knew it was important, but there was never enough space to get any more perspective than that.

As Dad began his dying process, I leaned into our ancestors for support. I wanted to believe that Dad would be welcomed with open arms—and maybe supported in his journey from where I would leave off. I imagined guiding him to the top step of a ladder, where someone else would reach out a hand from above to support him in taking that final leap of faith, that step off the ladder. I implored his parents, my grandparents, to be there for him. I thought especially of my grandmothers. About four days before Dad died, I was walking in the field behind our house before getting in the car to go see him. On the same hill where the rustling leaves often invoke my maternal grandmother's memory, I am sure that I heard both of my grandmothers giggling and excitedly exclaiming, "He's coming! It won't be long now." I knew he would be embraced when the energy of his life joined the universal energy of all that was and all that will be. I could let go. As I drove to visit that day, I felt a release. I suddenly felt like I was with Dad—or, more precisely, he was with me and would always be with me. His spirit had passed, and his body would be following soon behind. I knew he had peace, finally, and I had a peace and grateful joy swelling inside of me.

Yet less than an hour later, as I stood beside his laboring body, I was overcome by the sensations of his persistent life force. He was still there in tangible, finite form, just a shell of himself. I had felt his infinite presence, full and complete, abundant even, just an hour before while driving along the highway. Now standing next to his frail body gasping for air, I could attend only to the waning and struggling physical life force. In my confusion and grief, I seemed only able to know that particular moment as I sat holding his hand. I was caught in the discomfort of the dying and the letting go; I could not remember the joy and beauty of the eternal life that I had heard in my grandmothers' voices and felt in my body when Dad's presence joined me in the car. It took four more days for his body to quit this life and even longer for me to remember what I had known with great certainty the morning he actively began dying. He had already passed. His spirit would be with us always.

After Dad died, I was heartbroken and completely side-swiped. I felt like an earthquake had torn apart my world. All I could do was sit in wait and hope that the pieces would come back together. Eventually, slowly, they did. As I reviewed the new shape and form that materialized, I realized that I was forever changed. Life could not go back to the way it had been. I would always have the awareness that Dad had sharpened as he faded away. I would always know that our ancestors remain with us. I would remember that one life or one action to benefit another being benefits all life. This life that appears so finite and so complete is a snapshot of a whole that encompasses all past and future in this present moment.

I start my daily yoga practice as the night sky is just beginning to lighten. After building up the fire in the woodstove, I roll out my mat and stand erect with arms by my side in Mountain Pose (Tadasana). I face the glass door that leads to the field and opens to the horizon. I take a few deep breaths, feeling my feet settle into the earth; the muscles of my body engage and the chatter of my mind settles. This moment, before the sun has risen and the day has built its own momentum, is quiet, solitary, and full of potential. But this potential is not a beckoning toward the future; it is a fullness of the present. I take a few more deep breaths and feel my feet settle on the earth. I am grateful to be awake, in my body and fully receptive to this nascent moment. As I move through the sequence of sun salutations that open the practice, the sky lightens further.

By the time I am halfway through the standing sequence, strokes of color begin to travel across the sky. Oranges, pinks, and reds dance with the clouds in a constantly changing splash of color. I pause for a deep breath and a longer look.

With a grateful sigh, a smile, and a light heart, I return to the yoga practice after a minute or two. After all, I am supposed to be exercising. As I move through the poses, I feel my physical and mental energy grow stronger and more flexible. The growth builds throughout the practice each day, and each day's effort rests upon the work of the days, weeks, and months that came before. Yet each day's practice is also solely its own, complete with its own particular distractions, surprises, and sunrise.

Eventually, a rogue thought breaks my concentration and my gaze moves to the window again. Inevitably, a pang of surprise and disappointment sweeps through my body. The sun has risen above the horizon and the brilliant display that had filled the sky just moments before is gone. But of course it's gone. Nothing lasts forever. Change is our constant companion, usually accompanied by apprehension, awareness, and appreciation. This familiar truth takes me by surprise each and every time it presents itself.

The display of beauty cast by the interactions among sun, clouds, and earth is not only vibrant and awesome but also fragile and fleeting. Each time I witness this passing moment, I am surprised by a feeling of loss. The peak color display of the sunrise lasts ten to fifteen minutes, long enough to observe subtle changes and variations over time. Long enough to feel connected to and protected by the largesse of the universe. After the sun rises above the horizon, it is just me and my yoga mat again. I am sorry that the beauty of the sunrise is no longer with me. Its departure is a reminder of other losses and blessings that have graced my life.

But that moment passes too. A new moment has arrived, and it requires my attention. By this time, I am nearing the end of the sequence. In the final poses, I sink in with deep intention. Body, mind, and heart come together with strength, clarity, and integrity. As I move, I hold more lightly to the beauty and the loss of the sunrise and to countless other tender moments from past and future. Each pose requires only my body, my breath, and the universe's infinite possibility.

Return

)

To complete the mythic pattern, we not only have to return some of what we have received, we have to remember that we are always in the process of becoming. One way of looking at this is that we are always striving to get our will in harmony with the universal will.

—Robert Atkinson, *The Gift of Stories*

When Dad died, I sat down at my computer, intending to journal my way through the heartache of watching dementia interrupt his life and uproot mine. Through many words and many boxes of tissues, I discovered that my stories of grief, challenge, frustration, and joy were attached to reminders of what is most important. My writing revealed and polished a clarity of purpose. Although I had been caring *for* Dad, I was also receiving volumes of love *from* him. I observed tangible value in the time that we had spent together; it had given me a sense of deep purpose and connection. As I wrote, I rediscovered the same reciprocity and integrity that I had cultivated decades earlier while living and working in close relationship with the earth and my community. My first book, *Without a Map: A Caregiver's Journey through the Wilderness of Heart and Mind*, emerged from that writing.

Without a Map was an offering of love, companionship, and

compassion to other families making their way through challenging life circumstances. It also represented a step in a new direction. Through tears, sweat, edits, and fears, I shared a portion of my story with the world. Even so, I still find it hard to step fully into the author's role because I am not sure that I was wholly responsible for that book. It felt as though it was birthed out of me and, much like childbirth, I was only a vehicle. Gestating and birthing a baby is a miraculous experience. Gestating and birthing the book was as well—an act of grace as much as an act of will. *Without a Map* cracked open a door to authentic connection. As I continue to share the book and my story with others, I find new ways to reach into the sacred space that exists between all beings and reaffirm my commitment and connection to All That Is.

Living in connection to a world beyond what can be seen, touched, and felt is challenged by the pace, priorities, and restrictive language of our culture. Yet it is clear that a divine and infinite force flows through all life—including myself. This truth is what I circled around and what was being generously revealed to me in moments of wonder and grace throughout those seeking years. It was there in the moment of validation when I heard my grandfather's voice on the mountain. It was present in the peace that settled upon the boys and me at the beach and in the clarity of the dream when I released my grandmother from her earthly ties. It was there as I watched my father die. If there is a quality of my dad that persists beyond the confines of this life, then the same must be true of me, and of you, and of the earth.

I wanted to expand into this new awareness. To do so required me to seek out new language and new support.

A few months after Dad died, I applied to an interfaith ministry program. It seemed the perfect place to explore the "more" of life that had just come into view so clearly. The teachers, teachings, and classmates of that program became allies and resources for finding my way back into the world with the newly acknowledged gifts of awareness and connection. I explored a lot of questions, curious about what I believed in, what I had experienced in my life, and what the nature of my work in the world is. In the process, I examined the quest for the right people, place, and purpose that has undergirded my adult life. I began to wonder what my life story might teach me about my soul's intention in this lifetime. I imagined that, with new insight, I might be better able to manage the emerging events and aspects of my life to support that intention.

At this point, I had new guides. I was looking to ways of knowing from throughout human history. I was invited to use words, song, art, and movement to process new information and make it my own. In the religions and cultures of the world that I was being introduced and reintroduced to, I discovered mystics, prophets, and poets from across many cultures and generations whose insights resonated in my heart. As I studied their teachings and considered my own lived experience, I began to notice how familiar their knowing felt. Their wisdom seemed to mirror truths that I felt but could not name.

These were the truths that had been crystal clear in isolated moments: the wonder of connection at the spruce nursery, the peace that descended after the catharsis of throwing rocks at the beach, the knowing that if I didn't go outside, I would need a nap. I had, in fact, been in and out of napping for years. It was time to wake up; it was time to get outside. I did not need a literal return to the deep woods, I simply needed to honor my connection with the earth as my connection to the divine. I needed to celebrate the connection between the rhythms of the earth and the rhythms in my mind and heart. I needed to embrace the mutuality of my connections with all other beings, including humans, noticing and valuing the giving and receiving in each relationship. I had always sensed that there was something "more" to this life. Now I was ready to notice, name, and live into it more fully.

Studying the events of my own life in the mythic journey framework, I noticed two things. First, the call to adventure that led to my separation had actually always been a longing for connection. In the striving to find the "right" people, place, and purpose, I was hoping to know myself in relation to others. I was striving to regain our singularity, our oneness. Born into a time and place where individuality and competition were prized, I did not have the words or perspective to understand that my yearning was—and is—for interdependence and communion. My only yearning is to return to union with the Universal Spirit. When I recognized that, I understood my belonging to myself, too, and in a much more complete way.

Second, the hero's journey showed me that, even while I had been seeking, there had been moments of deep connection and clarity. These moments had arrived unbidden in dreams, in chance encounters, and in moments of awareness. In those moments I simply knew, with the kind of knowing that comes from the intuitive heart rather than the interpretive mind, that I was intimately connected to the same source that animates this living planet. In fact, the distinction between that source, the earth, and myself was arbitrary and illusory—a figment of our culture. I always have been and always will be an aspect of a larger divine whole. The messages have always been there and always will be. Now that I am aware of them, I pay greater attention.

As I go back into the cabin, I stoop to pick up a bobby pin on the threshold. I don't remember seeing it there a moment ago when I walked out the door. It isn't mine; I haven't worn bobby pins since my mom pulled my hair into a tight bun and fixed it with bobby pins and hair spray for ballet performances when I was very young. I pick it up and bring it inside. I place it on the bookshelf with the other tokens I have found on the threshold—a screw, a rusty nail, a paperclip, and a safety pin. I never find these things the first time I enter. My hands are always full of books, a lunch bag, and the single key that hangs on a soft green ribbon. That key is the gateway to the world of peace that the cabin holds for me.

Through the winter of remembering and writing about my call to adventure, the little cabin, tucked into the woods behind a friend's house, was a place of refuge and inspiration, a safe space in which to explore the meandering of my past and discover the lessons and opportunities I was meant to carry into the present. Over the season that I daydreamed and wrote and wondered there, I also found a handful of treasures.

These physical treasures mysteriously appeared on the threshold when I went to the outhouse or to the porch to get an armful of wood for the woodstove. They reminded me, usually when I needed it most, that I was not alone, and they reassured me that the universe was watching. Support was always available. The grounding force within my heart had backup from the divine. I was being nudged to remember and return to an eternal truth that I had somehow forgotten. Despite the myriad ways in which I felt separate, abandoned, and ignored by the world, it was becoming clearer and clearer that my way forward was to pay attention to the ways in which I am connected. The tokens of connection that appeared in my path—the nails, the safety pins, the other fasteners—were reminders to pay closer attention to the interconnectedness of my life, and to use my life to build and strengthen connectivity. My connections to myself, to other people, and to the earth are ultimately the lived expression of oneness with the Universal Spirit that unites us all. It is here now. It has always been here. It will always be here.

Stepping into connection with deep intention has brought me back into the human family in an incredible way. I feel my sense of responsibility to myself, to others, and to the whole. As one body in a complex interwoven system, I have a responsibility to participate. That translates into a desire to share my story and hold space for others to share their stories. For me, that has meant stepping toward those points of connection to offer what I have and to learn what they have to teach. As I move into deepening relationships with the communities—natural and human—in which I live, I believe that I move closer to expressing the divine nature of this human experience while also inviting others closer to theirs.

A Call to Wholeness
Remembering

Both And

I am part
Rising with the sun
Falling with the rain
Unfolding with the crocus
Waning with the moon
Dying with the leaves.

I am whole
Spreading light and heat
Weeping tears on hardpan ground
Holding lightly to beauty and hope
Contracting into darkness
Withering in despair before
Rising in hope once again.

With new awareness and clear intention, I turned to the living earth and the small, still voice inside of myself. Living into my own emerging awareness in this way has helped me to step toward my purpose with enhanced focus and attention. My purpose, in fact, seems to require me to stop seeking and to dig in more deeply to the here and now. My purpose, really, is simply to be grounded in this place and time. From here, I can offer the work of my heart and the work of my hands to the healing of our world, one moment at a time.

While the hero's journey provided a mythic framework for reflecting on the patterns of earlier life experiences, the seasons provide a framework for observing my ongoing spiritual development and deepening participation in the web of creation. I am particularly attentive to the external and internal light and energy at the cross-quarter days, the halfway points between each equinox and solstice. With a wise and sprightly friend, I co-created a series of seasonal celebrations for a local nonprofit that seeks to invite individuals and organizations into the healing and sustaining rhythms of the natural world. As we plan our gatherings, we lean into observations and stories from a variety of world traditions. Steeped in the myths and practices that have sustained cultures for generations, I recognize my experience of the seasons as part of a lineage that extends both backward and forward across time and place. After all, the Wabanaki, the ancestral inhabitants of my current homespace, and my European ancestors who lived at a similar line of latitude would have noticed and responded to the subtle shifts of light, energy, and temperature throughout the year in similar ways. While participating in these Seasonal Celebrations, I remember my belonging and role within a wider and deeper web of both humanity and ecology.

Paying attention to the seasonal cycles has drawn me to reconnect with the wisdom of the earth. The natural world has always inspired and guided me, but now, as I pay closer attention, I see the sacred that is revealed in the everyday with greater clarity and ease. Specifically, I notice the numinous moments that arrive unbidden and when I least expect them. And, joyfully, I notice them much more often. Instead of brilliant moments of clarity and glimpses of eternity arriving every few years, they arrive regularly. They have probably always been here with great frequency, I have just been too distracted to notice or embrace them. As I pay more attention to these moments, I am reclaiming my relationship with the divine and stepping into my responsibility to contribute positively to the unfolding stories around me.

Writing my reflections and observations helps ground my intention to pay closer attention. In harmony and presence with all that is, I remember my true nature. My body is a small casement that holds the possibility of the boundless infinite. As an aspect of the Universal Spirit, I am both earth and spirit bound by flesh and blood. We all are! The idea fills me with awe and humility and, I'm surprised to notice, does not fill me with panic. I do not feel a heavy weight of responsibility with this awareness. There is a levity. I know that I am enough. Here. Now. Enough.

I also know that I am here for a reason. I am assured that I belong to this time and this place. I am sinking deeply into this one precious life, loving its singularity and its universality and intending to live each of its moments fully. I trust that I have a contribution to make and that I have arrived just in time to offer it.

Summer Solstice

The garden has responded to the rain, heat, and light by leaping. The kale has spread its wings. The tomato plants have grown long, gangly limbs. The asparagus continues to grow by inches each day. There is more than we can eat and our neighbors are appreciating the overflow.

The trees hold the raindrops on their leaves. When the wind blows, the excess shakes off. As I run under the thick canopy, the trees weep on me. Big drops of liquid roll off the edges of the leaves and onto my head. Their release is my anointing this morning.

Today is the summer solstice, the longest day and shortest night in our hemisphere. It is cloudy and rainy, so we may not see the rays of the sun today, but its presence is palpable in the fertility that surrounds us. This is a time of great abundance—abundant light, abundant rain, a beautiful full moon. There is abundance in my heart, too. Abundant joy and peace in my daily moments with my family and abundant sorrow when I extend my awareness to the human family and the wider earth. Like the trees, weighted by the rain, I shed the excessive abundance in tears that leak from the corners of my eyes. I insist on loving, laughing, and learning despite the losses, aching, and dismay. The only way to hold the weight of it all, these two extremes, is to throw my arms wide open and settle in.

Paddling

I paddle slowly to the middle of the lake, loosely following the path of the three herons who passed overhead moments earlier. At the water's surface, turtle heads emerge and disappear without rhythm or sound. Periodic percussive slaps interrupt the silence as fish leap for insects. Standing on the paddleboard, surrounded by the company of the morning lake, I drift in and out of thoughts and thoughtlessness, at one with the other beings of the lake. My paddle becomes a prayer of thanks as I fall into gratitude for my place in this world. Turning to head toward home, my prayer anchors to both past and future.

Thomas sits on the pier, settled in his own version of solitary morning prayer. But, to my sight, he does not seem to be alone. My great-grandmother, who died years before I was born, is with him on the pier. My father, grandfather, and uncle, more recently gone from this life, are there too. Dozens of others whom I do not recognize are there. Certainly there are more people than would fit on the pier if they were in physical form. On the bank behind them, my grandmother who died nine years ago sits on a bench surrounded by flowers. She is overcome with emotion, reveling in love of nature and family, exclaiming the wonder of it all with the generous tears and laughter that always flowed together. She always marveled at the miracle of our lives. Now I understand her awe. With past, present, and future blending together, we are left speechless, without the words to explain the knowing and the not-knowing that accompany our experience of reality. Tears and laughter sum up the rich fullness of it all but I can't resist the urge to try to understand in words.

A week ago, I had the opportunity to begin to share *Without a Map: A Caregiver's Journey through the Wilderness of Heart and Mind* with audiences through presentations and signings. I offered a glimpse of what I had learned from accompanying

Dad during his decline with dementia. I also communicated my vision of a world in which we all step in close with one another, in reciprocal connection and compassion. I invited the attendees to envision the generations of people who had come before us, both giving and receiving care, and encouraged them to lean into the generous teachings of those generations. As each one of us steps into the symbiotic relationships in our own lives, we will see ourselves as part of a single interconnected whole.

In Bob Atkinson's book *The Story of Our Time: From Duality to Interconnectedness to Oneness*, he describes these personal actions of connectivity as examples of the evolution of human consciousness, an evolution that is both inevitable and supported by our intentional actions. He asks, "Wouldn't our greatest act in this world be to express love, compassion, caring, and charity in all things we do? Understanding the path to our own evolution means awakening to our own humanity, to the specialness that is ours only."

In that light, my call to connection is also a call to participate actively in a personal and collective turn toward fulfilling our potential. Paddling back to the pier where my husband, ancestors, and descendants are waiting, I am reminded that forever is here now. It is also yesterday and yesterday's yesterday—and tomorrow and tomorrow's tomorrow. In gratitude and connection, I glide across the water, brimming with love and wonder. I am the shy turtle, the boisterous fish, and the graceful herons all at once. I am speechless, but my heart is light and I am laughing through my tears.

Dry? Freeze? Jam? Give Thanks.

The gifts of summer have filled my senses to overflowing.

The air is warm but not hot and is constantly refreshed by a gentle breeze that keeps the bugs at bay. Recently, the wind has carried either the thick, fecund smell of cow manure or a floral smell with origins we can't identify. This morning, I woke to the drumming of a gentle steady rain. Other mornings, it is the call of birds that pulls me from sleep. They are declaring territory or announcing food rather than calling for mates as they were a few months ago. The flowers and butterflies are a kaleidoscope of colors, changing from one day to the next as they blossom, mature, and decline. The garden is overflowing with fragrant herbs, and this short growing season's crops are at their peak. What am I to do with this abundance?

I begin the day trying to rein in the bounty. I cut handfuls of herbs, attempting to save their fresh flavor for the long winter ahead. We built a new drying rack this year and strung a line inside. I am excited to be able to preserve some of the fragrance and flavor for later days. But I am not fooled. I know the dried herbs will be more subdued than the fresh ones that we put in our salad last night. While it will be nice to have the herbs from our garden in a winter soup as a reminder of summer, they will not bring back the sensory extravagance of the season.

And what about the ten pounds of local blueberries I ordered? We have eaten our fill and shared with friends. I need to preserve what's left before they begin to rot. We can freeze some for winter smoothies and baked goods. But the freezer is still full of the strawberries that we picked in July. It will have to be jam and blueberry muffins and blueberry pancakes and— Wait!

Over the course of the morning, I have gone from fully enjoying the season's bounty to attempting to preserve it for future enjoyment to struggling to find ways to use it lest there be waste. I want to be a good steward of the earth's resources, but I don't mean to be clinging to this bounty. I am painfully aware of inequity in the world and always carry the heavy burden of responsibility along with the awareness of my good fortune at being able to maintain the safety and health of my family. But somehow the preservation of the season's excess has started to feel greedy—protecting the harvest so I can have it tomorrow, too.

The better response to the season's joys is gratitude. Weeks ago, I realized that I could not harness the indulgence of the late, lazy mornings or the giggly late nights of my teenage boys enjoying the freedoms of an unencumbered summer together. I have stopped expecting them to wake up at a reasonable hour and do something (anything). Now, I am waiting patiently for them to greet the day and join me on an adventure in the late morning. I expect them to support the household in basic ways, but I also enjoy treating them like the children they were, pouring their tea or first cup of milk in the morning. I listen to their late-night antics with a smile, even when they are keeping me awake. I know it won't last. Future summers will have work obligations, academic goals, or other distractions. Or maybe they won't. Either way, they won't be this one.

The same is true in the garden and the kitchen. I will preserve the excess fruits of the summer season, but I cannot retain summer. And I don't really want to. I want to harvest today's abundance and store enough to meet tomorrow's needs without holding too tight. I want to celebrate the smells, tastes, sounds, and sights of this day. Preservation for the future is important, but gratitude for the present nourishes even more deeply. Summer's abundance will soon be gone, but autumn will be full of gifts too. We can welcome each season with joy and preserve its abundance with a gentle hand and light heart. As these long days of summer begin to wane, I will dry, jam, freeze, and share the season's fruits and vegetables. And, most importantly, I will give thanks.

Blueberry Hill

On many Sunday mornings, I attend a Quaker meeting. Gathering in the bright, sunny meeting room for an hour of silent worship is incredibly nourishing. In that space and time, stillness settles in and I feel myself one with All That Is. No words necessary. Even if I leave after the rise of meeting without speaking a word to anyone, I always leave feeling deeply grounded, present to my life as it is unfolding, and thoroughly connected to the community. Some days this sense of presence and connection grows into a sense of urgency to respond to the needs of the world. Other days, it blossoms into a sense of being warmly held, not just by the immediate community but by the entire web of life. Always, it feeds my spirit.

This morning, as soon as I wake up, I know I will not go to meeting. The sun is shining, a breeze is blowing, and I know the blueberries on the hill are ripe and ready to be picked. With a steaming cup of coffee in one hand and an empty bowl in the other, I walk into the morning sun to harvest the sweet fruits. As my bowl slowly fills, my mind quiets and my heart is at peace. *I am at meeting after all.* Only here, instead of gathering with human family, I am in communal worship with the breeze, the sun, the fruits at my feet, the bugs buzzing in my ears, the muscles in my back and legs, the deer and turkeys who grazed here earlier this morning, the birds singing from the nearby branches, the ancestors who brought me here, and all the humans over time who have gathered their breakfast in warm summer sun.

I go inside just long enough to make blueberry pancakes and then bring them outside to eat. As flavors of blueberry, maple, and pancake melt in my mouth, I am overwhelmed by a sense of gratitude. What an amazing gift it is to be alive to relish this sweetness on my tongue, the sun on my face, and the chorus of birds. Right next to all of the burdens and responsibilities of this time and place, amid all of its challenges and uncertainties and the work to be done, there is this: beauty and abundance, peace and presence, community and connection—all ready for harvest in my backyard and in my heart.

Next week we celebrate Lammas, the festival of the harvest in Celtic tradition. At the midpoint between the summer solstice and the fall equinox, the harvest is in full swing. Life and death stand side by side: fruits are ripening as stalks are dying. We are called to notice and honor the value of both creation and destruction, disintegration and integration. Holding the paradox can be uncomfortable. It requires stretching, strength, and trust in our own capacity. It requires practice, and it requires taking breaks for solace in whatever ways I can. Sometimes the solace finds me. This morning, peace was waiting on Blueberry Hill. Where will it find me next?

Lammas

To celebrate Lammas (a.k.a. Lughnasa or Harvest Festival), the midway point between the summer solstice and the fall equinox, I gather with a group in a community garden overlooking a meadow with waist-high grass and insects and birds of all colors and songs. Standing in witness to this abundance, we honor the complexity of our world. We pause to notice both the shrinking hours of daylight and the bounty of the harvest. We have time and space to take it all in, to pay attention to the miracles of life that bring us here together—with one another and with the gifts of the season.

After an introduction that invites us into our awe, we reflect on all we are grateful for and take turns naming those elements to the group. One attendee gives thanks for the dust of exploding stars that are the original source of the iron that courses through our bodies. Another person gives thanks to the biome within our guts that maintains the health of our bodies. Another acknowledges the teachers, the ancestors, and the wisdom-keepers who have ensured that the literal and figurative seeds of life continue from generation to generation. Each individual expression of gratitude is an invitation to all assembled to pay attention to that particular piece of the intricate web of connection, if only for a few moments.

When it is my turn, I offer gratitude for my children. My commitment to nurture and nourish them is simply part of my commitment to nurture and nourish all life—and the land and water that will sustain it. By their presence, my children guide me toward just and compassionate actions and words. I am grateful for the daily reminder to notice and honor my responsibility to the wider web of creation.

I often notice gratitude and responsibility nesting together and guiding my actions as I tend to the myriad details and relationships that crosshatch each day. I frequently repeat a series of vows that Joanna Macy shares in *Active Hope*. The affirmation captures my sense of responsibility to this time and place and clarifies my intention to live in an honoring and sustaining way.

> I vow to myself and to each of you:
>
> To commit myself daily to the healing of our world and the welfare of all beings.
>
> To live on the earth more lightly and less violently in the food, products and energy I consume.
>
> To draw strength and guidance from the living Earth, the ancestors, the future beings and my brothers and sisters of all species.
>
> To support each other in our work for the world and to ask for help when I feel the need.
>
> To pursue a daily practice that clarifies my mind, strengthens my heart and supports me in observing these vows.

As we approach the fall equinox, I am paying close attention. I am curious to see what new awareness arises in the balance between dark and light, warm and cool. Whatever emerges, I will greet it with gratitude and responsibility.

If You Need a Reminder

The field seems to be steaming as the night's rain evaporates and mixes with the humidity hanging heavily in the air. Adding to the density in the air, the birds are busy in both flight and song. Mesmerized, I walk toward the pond, startling a gaggle of chatty geese into the air. It is beautiful and lush, but the fecundity is almost overwhelming. My pace, typically slow and thoughtful, begins to feel plodding and heavy—almost tentative. And that's when I notice. I am a full participant in the intricate web of life in the field. There has been a mosquito hatch, and the hungry young insects have found me!

I recall advice that a friend offered many years ago when we were paddling in the Boundary Waters Canoe Area Wilderness. She reminded me of how much we humans take from the earth and how little tangible positive benefit we offer back to her. In that context, feeding a few mosquitoes is really not too much to ask. She suggested that we honor each bug by treating each bite as an offering rather than a violation. But instead of assuming some equilibrium or a Buddha-like mind while enjoying my long walk through the field, content to serve a feast to some of the tiny insects that provide a critical foundation to the food chain, I turn around and hustle back up the trail. I even kill a few mosquitoes as I approach my car.

That evening, without cause or a point of origin, I am over-whelmed by sadness about the hurt in the world. The weight of my grief is relieved by a good, long cry. Sometimes it is simply too much to hold gratitude for my safety, health, and loved ones while also bearing witness to the suffering that we are inflicting on one another and on the earth. A good cry helps. A long walk in the field usually does, too.

Was my grief overload triggered by my hasty retreat and the mosquitoes I had mindlessly killed, or was it just time to let off some steam?

I don't know. But I do know that I feel better. And I know that the mosquitoes are hungry and we are food. There is a lesson in there somewhere. While I wait to find out what it is, I will continue to work on gently expanding my compassionate heart.

If You Need a Reminder

If you need a reminder that
>Your blood, sweat, and tears matter
>And that your compassion will be tested ...

If you need a reminder that
>You are the only *you* the world will ever know ...

If you need a reminder
>That you are significant ...

Take a walk
In a steamy summer field after the rains have stopped.
>The flowers will be lifting their heads to the sun,
>While the birds dry their wings and
>Thousands of newly hatched mosquitoes wait for their first meal.
>Each one offers a powerful reminder.

Standing with a Heron

I took off my shoes before setting out on the trail this morning. My transient thoughts are easily replaced by the simple pleasures of wet earth beneath my feet, changing seasons in the air, and glimpses of butterflies. While the river on the horizon and the vast field in front of me suggest a faraway place, the hum of the freeway and the horn of a passing train remind me that I am just outside of town. I am only taking a quick walk between two meetings.

Rounding the bend that turns me back toward the parking lot, my gaze falls on a heron. He is standing just a few yards off the path in a muddy patch of the field. He is not hunting; there isn't any water nearby and his gaze is loose, not fixed. He is just standing, the way herons do—strong, silent, still. Motionless, he beckons me to join him.

Grateful for the invitation, I know I will stay as long as he will have my company.

I reach for my phone, hoping to capture our shared time, thinking I can save the experience to appreciate again another day or share with someone else. I take a video of his graceful and sturdy presence until my phone runs out of storage space. When it does, I put my phone away quickly, knowing it could not possibly capture this moment and embarrassed that I had held my little screen between us.

With relief, I give myself more fully to the heron, to my standing, and to our shared stillness. Meeting his quiet presence with my body, mind, and heart, I stand in stillness with him until we are no longer two creatures standing in a field. We are clearly one with each other and with the field. We stand, in this oneness, for several minutes.

Finally, the heron turns to walk away. He takes a few deliberate and patient long-legged steps toward the river before pausing again for just a slight moment longer. Maybe he moved because the sun was in his eyes or maybe it was lunchtime ... or maybe he had heron business to attend to elsewhere. Whatever the reason, his movement brings me back to my human body, standing in a moist field on a mid-September morning. I need to be moving along also. After all, I have human business to attend to. The day promised to include dozens of the concerns that a human life carries. I had not planned for it to include long moments with a heron.

As I turn to continue along the path, a pale purple butterfly flies off my left foot. Apparently, she had joined our meditation too. Her delicate levity offers the perfect balance to the heron's gravity.

Walking away, I am grateful for the invitation to pause and join the heron so fully that the mirage of our separateness dissolved completely for a moment. I am grateful for the presence of creatures who remind me that we are one. And I am grateful that these moments, though always with me and within me, come to find me when I need them most.

As I step off the trail and into my shoes and my next commitment, I hold gently to the heron's stillness, the butterfly's levity, the wet earth at my feet, and the gentle breeze. May I carry their clarity and presence into my work and relationships. May I invite others into that peace that connects us all. May the embrace of stillness forever delight.

Lupine Patch

Another day, another barefoot walk. This time I am circling the "lupine patch" in the middle of our backyard. We mow around this jumble of wild field every year, leaving a circular oasis of weedy pasture that becomes a safe bedroom for deer and turkeys and a bountiful pantry for birds, bees, and butterflies.

Examining the patch, I notice a monarch chrysalis. Finally! I have seen a lot of monarch butterflies this summer but very few caterpillars and no chrysalises. Here is a dazzling green chrysalis with gold flecks hanging from a tall stem of grass. As I step in to look more closely, I notice another and another and another. Two have already been vacated: they are transparent hollow shells. Another is dark, so close to emergence that the wings of the butterfly inside are visible.

Thatcher calls from the other side of the patch. "I think I see a butterfly that just came out!" As I look up, a butterfly takes flight. "I think we saw his first flight," Thatcher explains. "He was standing right next to that empty chrysalis drying his wings when I first saw him."

As we watch the butterfly fly off, something lifts in me. Continuing to walk around the circle and noticing more chrysalises at various stages, I think about strength and resilience. Just a few years ago, we had worried that the population of monarchs was declining. I am not sure about the worldwide population of monarchs, but here in my backyard they are healthy and plentiful. I think about transitions and transformation and wonder about the human capacity for change. If humans are caterpillars, how many of us are still too busy eating to see what's coming, only paying attention to the bite of leaf in front of us? How many of us are stuck as if in chrysalis form, ready to burst and join others who are already aloft with wings of compassion and care? How many individuals need to transform before a tidal shift can occur? If humans were monarchs, where would I fit in this process of change?

When I began to walk around the lupine patch, I had been sad for days, carrying a grief that I couldn't name or really understand. I hadn't felt compelled to pinpoint my grief. After all, loss feels ubiquitous these days. The web of life has been stretched and stressed until the planet and all of its inhabitants are suffering. I did not need to explore in practical detail the myriad ways in which loss of life, dignity, sovereignty, and potential are reflected in my own temporary losses of safety, hope, joy, and courage. I had just been allowing myself to feel it—noticing its heaviness and vagueness. I trusted that the grief had work to do in me and that it would lift when I was ready.

I am ready when I remember to reconnect with the living earth around me. With the resilient earth beneath my feet, my imagination takes flight with the butterflies and I remember. I remember that we are all one. I remember that the magnificent capacity for change and healing that I witness in the earth also exists within each one of us. I remember that I am a co-creator—yesterday, today, and tomorrow. Today, I choose transformation.

Fall Equinox

Each fall, even as the squash continues to grow out of the garden bed, sending its long tendrils into the yard, I begin to clean and clear the abundant plant growth that is dying back in other beds. The lettuce bolted long ago, and the kale is turning rubbery. As I remove dead and dying stalks from some of the beds, I turn the soil, mixing the layers of humus, redistributing nutrient-rich organic matter to different depths. Some of the plant matter goes to the compost pile so it can break down more thoroughly before being returned to the garden as soil another year.

There is some sadness to the end of the growing season, but there is relief as well. I need a break, an opportunity to slow down and take stock. The season invites a slowing down. This is not a retreat (yet). It is simply a change of pace and a shift in perspective.

Fall flowers are blooming in the field. The air is full of bird-song as the migrators traveling south join the residents for a spell. The butterflies continue to emerge from their chrysalises. I wonder if they will have time to mate and lay eggs before the cold hits. If they do, what will become of the eggs that hatch? Is there enough time for the caterpillars to eat, grow, transform within the hardened shell of their chrysalises, and emerge as butterflies to mate again? As I walk the field and find monarchs at all different stages, I wonder how they know to pause their northern life cycle in order to migrate south and avoid the cold, hard frost.

I also wonder how I will know to pause. Even in this season when summer's abundance is waning, in the garden and in my mind, I busy myself with preparation for the seasons ahead. In this season, I too am turning over. As I sift through the past and seek to claim the present with intention, there is a lot to digest. The plant matter that has been added to the compost pile is broken down into nutrient-rich soil by sunlight, moisture, and heat. Likewise, old beliefs and ways of knowing are transformed. Picking up and noticing each experience or emotion, I can offer whatever is necessary to myself and to the circumstance. Some memories seem to need an offering of gratitude, compassion, or forgiveness. Most, however, simply ask to be acknowledged. As each arises and I offer it my attention, it moves out of my body and into my hand—into the kaleidoscope that I have built out of the colors and distortions of my past. In my hand, the kaleidoscope adds light, color, and perspective to new experiences.

As I observe memories and emotions that arrive, dissolve, and reemerge, I hold myself and the process gently. Like the monarchs, I will simply continue in motion, trusting in the unfolding processes within me and within the world around me.

To Dad, with Love

I have been missing you. At the same time, I feel you in our lives every day. The gifts of the time that we shared resonate in me. When I look at the sky, I remember the reverence with which you gazed to the horizon. When I walk, I remember long walks we had together and your appreciation for the motion and clarity that they brought. When my family is chaotic, I remember how that once entertained you and later overwhelmed you. We have all continued to grow tremendously since you died, but I sense that would not surprise you. You supported, nurtured, and nudged throughout your life, and even as you died. Thank you for letting us stay close.

Your last weeks and days touched a deep and unknown place in me and connected me with a sense of spirit beyond our knowing. Perhaps this is what is referred to in the Christian tradition as the "Holy Spirit." I can only call it a mystery, the great unknown, perhaps even the divine—but "divine" sounds so pleasant and this depth of life's continuum holds tremendous sorrow as well as great joy. I waited years for grace to intervene in your situation. I kept thinking that it was unfair that you should suffer, hoping that grace would usher your spirit from the body that was holding you hostage in this time and place. Ultimately, grace was slow—and not all that graceful. But perhaps there was a teaching, a gift, in that experience for you. There was for me.

Since you left, I have been soul-searching, literally. As I scour my soul for the pieces that exist beyond time, space, and body, I find love, patience, kindness, hope. It bears a striking similarity to the essence that I saw in you. I am participating in an interfaith ministry program to help me uncover the truths that I can know about myself and the world and to identify how I can support the world. When you died, I noticed how much time and space I had reserved in my days for us to be together. Filling that time with this program, I am continuing the learning that I began with you. I dedicate myself to growing my understanding and commitment to that small, still voice inside of me. At this moment it whispers, and I need to attend to it carefully to make sure it gets airtime in our noisy, busy lives. As I give it love and attention, that voice will grow louder and stronger. For it is not really *my* voice, it is the expression of the spirit that comes through me. I am dedicating time and energy to clearing the pathways for its manifestation. It is hard work. Not unlike walking through the last few years with you, I have no idea what I am doing. I will just take one step at a time and trust the process. While it is easy to say that, it is hard to do it. I am anxious, wanting to make the most of this opening in me, afraid that somehow the door may close if I don't get through in time, afraid that this opportunity will work around me rather than through me. As I write it, I know that is silly. Yes, time moves, opportunities come and go, people come and go. The cycle is a circle, but the work of the spirit beyond me will persist; in fact, it will persist through me.

You walked me into my life, and you walked me into this opening. I am profoundly grateful. I feel you supporting, loving, and nurturing as I keep inching along. Thank you.

To John Muir, with Gratitude

John Muir (1838–1914) was a writer, naturalist, and social activist. I discovered his writing in the months after my first trip into the wilderness. I was sixteen and on a six-week camping trip. That trip was my first close encounter with high peaks, deep wilderness, and the essence that percolates beyond the realm of the physical. Nothing in my life to that point had ever hinted toward the ethereal—not that I had noticed anyway. I had grown up regularly attending an Episcopal church and Sunday school and, at the time, was attending a Catholic high school. I had an appreciation for the formality and traditions of religion, but I had never felt anything that could be called spirituality. I'm not sure that I had even recognized that it was absent. I had heard the concept and even thought that I believed in its existence, but I had never experienced it.

In the mountains, I felt a oneness that was surely the holiness I had heard described in church. I turned the corner at the end of a long switchback and emerged above the tree line. An immense valley opened below me, the wide sky stretched above me, and I felt myself melt into the expanse. I didn't know what it was, but I felt it, I loved it, and I was loved by it. I didn't need to believe it or understand it; I *knew* it. I became devoted to honoring and protecting Mother Earth.

In the months after my trip, I began reading John Muir, and his words helped me to embrace and touch the sensation more fully. I took many armchair journeys as I pored over his adventures. With a naturalist's training and an artist's heart, Muir described the glory, wonder, ferocity, and peace of moving among trees, storms, creeks, and mountain peaks. His words resonated with my experience of the wilderness and, perhaps even more importantly, with the spirituality that my travels had awakened in me. He captured the interconnection vividly: "We are now in the mountains and they are in us, kindling enthusiasm, making every nerve quiver, filling every pore and cell of us."

In sentence after sentence about forests, mountains, and glaciers, Muir validated my budding awareness that I was connected to a larger whole. He linked my fragile teenage humanity to the vast and mighty natural world. He acknowledged all of nature as God. Reading his essays was like a walk through an old-growth forest dripping with sights, sounds, and feelings. He was an accomplished alpinist and a risk-taker, so rapt by experience that his own health and safety were quite secondary. He spent many months living simply and closely to the earth, alone or with just a few others in wild places. Through his words and sketches, you would believe that he was most happy with the trees and birds for neighbors, but he was also passionately committed to protecting wild spaces.

I relished his observations and the conclusion that there is more for us to glean from wilderness than just an understanding of the sum of the parts. Wild spaces and humans are expressions of the same spirit. We need one another. Muir observed that "the tendency nowadays to wander in wilderness is delightful to see. Thousands of tired, nerve-shaken, over-civilized people are beginning to find out that going to the mountains is going home; that wilderness is a necessity; and that mountain parks and reservations are useful not only as fountains of timber and irrigating rivers, but as fountains of life."

While Muir advocated that people get out into wilderness

whenever possible, he also argued that it is important for us to know that wild places exist even if we can't get there. His love of wild spaces both for their own sake and for their potential to heal humanity fueled his persistence; his writing and lobbying ultimately contributed to the development of the National Park Service. As I learned more about John Muir, his activism sparked mine.

In the decades since my first encounter with wilderness, my connection to nature has grounded, guided, and supported me. Muir's stories kept my passion for the wilderness alive while I was making my way through college, suburbs, and cities, and I followed his advice to "keep close to Nature's heart … and break clear away once in a while, and climb a mountain or spend a week in the woods. Wash your spirit clean." For a few years, I stepped off the beaten path quite fully, living off the grid and close to the earth. In those years, the rhythms of my days closely followed the rhythms of the sun, moon, seasons, and critters.

I didn't see it at the time, but I now fully recognize that my forays into wilderness, my inclination to keep my hands in the dirt, and my connection to seasonal cycles have been my link to a Universal Spirit all this time. I named my affinity to Mother Earth; Muir named his to God's creation. We were talking about the same thing. Renamed and reclaimed, the thread of nature that has been running through my life is already being woven into new patterns.

The Divine Speaks
The Divine speaks
In rustling leaves and
Babbling brooks.
In singing birds and
Howling wolves,
The Divine speaks.

The Divine glows
In oranges, pinks, and purples

Of the rising and setting sun.
In the brilliant white reflection
Of the full moon
The Divine glows.

The Divine lives
In wind and earthworm,
Mountain and valley.
In you and me,
Eagle and salmon.
The Divine lives.

Shifting Sands

Yesterday afternoon I sat in class for three hours. We talked about stillness, meditation, and prayer. My energy rose and fell as the conversation ebbed and flowed. I was introspective, drawn inward rather than outward by the conversation, but I was also restless. Across the circle, a friend caught my eye and I recognized that I had been fidgeting anxiously with my feet. An hour later, I emerged from the womb of that basement classroom full of other souls following their own journeys of the heart. Leaving, like birthing, felt unsettling. In our three hours together, we had fallen deeply into being there in that birthing space together. Taking leave of it, I was acutely aware of again entering the unknown of the wide world.

Crossing the road to get to my car, I noticed how fast the passing cars were going. The mist made the air heavy and dim; it seemed too early to be dusk. It was too loud, too fast, and too dark for me to absorb. When I got to the car, my phone erupted with notifications of text messages and missed calls. A massive earthquake had hit in Mexico, not far from where Duncan was living and going to school. Duncan, his classmates, and his host family were safe and their home was undamaged, but they were all shaken. My trembling heart echoed the trembling earth. Again, it hit me how fluid and unpredictable this life is. How can there be time or space for rest and stillness? The sand is always shifting beneath our feet.

After the momentary panic of awareness, I returned to the nexus of our conversation about stillness, prayer, and meditation. Those practices percolate from deep within us and, more importantly for me, from a space beyond knowing and thought. Practicing them with intention prepares us to respond from a well that is deeper than our own experiences. Drawing from beyond time, space, and body, we can find abundant strength, courage, and love to give and release. Stillness, meditation, and prayer nourish us from a well that is always available—the limitless expanse where Love, Spirit, Mystery, God, Goddess, Allah, Divine resides. It is from this deep well of constancy that we may be better able to receive and release life's external comings and goings with something that resembles grace.

Today I write the following as an invitation for the beginning of next week's class:

Come in, friends. There is a storm outside.

The earth will not stop trembling while we pause, but we will find stillness here. In this room, we are held and nourished, stimulated and refreshed. We need only glance around this circle to witness the light of divine love—or close our eyes and feel its tender warmth.

In this room, our flame may flicker in the wind and then grow brighter. We may doubt and then feel our resolve grow stronger. Our love may wiggle and waver, but we trust that it will persist. The sacred womb of this room prepares each of us to boldly carry that love like a torch into the night. And we find that they are one and the same together, the womb that holds us and the one that wells up from a knowing deep within each of us.

In a lifetime during which nothing lasts and the ground will always move beneath our feet, take refuge here. We are both holding and always held. Be still. Welcome.

Samhain

At Samhain (*SA-win*) the days are getting shorter. Darkness arrives in the late afternoon and the sun peeks over the horizon later and later each morning. Outdoor chores have become minimal. The plants in the garden have gone dormant and the ground is frozen so there is no gardening to do. The snow has not yet begun to fall so there is no shoveling to do. When the sun is shining, long afternoon walks are crisp and inviting. When the cold rain falls, it is easier to sit by the woodstove and daydream, read, or knit. This season seems to be made for resting, for waiting. The impulse to be productive is dulled and the urge to reflect is insistent.

It is said that, at this time, the veil between the living and the dead is thin. Between October 30 and November 1, rituals in a number of traditions invite remembrance and celebration of the dead. Celebrating the end of the harvest season, the growing season of darkness, and the spiritual journeys of those who have died, I am drawn into ever-deeper retreat and contemplation. I pay extra attention to the world around me and how it resonates in my heart. I am looking, listening, and smelling more than usual for bits of wisdom, comfort, or warning that arrive mysteriously and hold a hint of the eternal.

Oak Leaf

It has been windy. Most of the leaves have now fallen from the trees, and remnants of the yellow and red flames of autumn are turning brown in the hollow spaces alongside the roads and fields. Ditches and culverts have filled with their excess and the rainwater must find new paths through and around the piles of decaying vegetation. Taking a walk early one afternoon, I feel the shift in the seasons settle into my bones and suggest a pause to my busy mind. The fecundity and fullness of spring and summer have given way to the barren openness of late fall. This is the time for hibernating, resting, waiting, and attending.

But there is so much to do. How can I possibly pause amid the great need and my longing for a safer, gentler world?

The air is crisp and still. The only obvious motion, besides me, comes from a half-dozen juncos and a lone cardinal that dart from bush to tree and back again. Out of the corner of my eye, I spot an oak leaf falling. I stop to watch it spiral slowly toward the ground. The leaf has strength and integrity, but it falls with a gentle lightness. The only leaf in sight, it seems so solitary and yet so much a part of both sky and earth.

Looking around for the host tree from which it fell and not finding any candidates, I realize it must have drifted quite a distance before beginning its downward dance. Yet there is no wind, not that I can sense anyway. A breeze more subtle than anything I could perceive carried it aloft from its tree to the middle of this open field. Yet it was carried, strong and sure, to the place before me.

I must trust that I will be held by that which I cannot see.

Picking it up, I study the sturdy oak leaf. It is a uniform shade of brown. Each lobe is unbroken, its edges sharp. Complete and intact, the leaf is so perfect that it could be an end to itself. Yet here it is so clearly playing a part in a larger cycle of life. Through the spring and summer, this leaf nourished and strengthened the tree. Now, in autumn, it has fallen to the ground, where sun, rain, and insects will turn it into nutrient-rich soil, bedding for new roots in next year's growing cycle. Letting go of its place on the branch, it falls to the ground and finds new purpose creating space for new life.

I must release what is to allow for what is to come.

Laying the leaf back down on the field, I know it will become one of many when the wind picks up and gathers the stray leaves together in piles. No longer singular, each leaf becomes truly part of the chorus of living, dying, and decaying material. When spring comes bursting forth, this bed of leaves will be host to the insects, seeds, and roots of new life. But first, there will be snow.

I must rest now. There is a potential unfolding.

Winter's rest is a gestation, a period of rapid development taking place out of sight and intent. As I embrace the longest nights and shortest days of the year, the darkness invites me to pay attention to a subtle growth. I must hold my impatient, active, and eager "doing" self aside to make space for my allowing, accepting, and "receiving" self.

It is time to stand in a clearing.

In the Clearing
This year, in this season, I am practicing standing gratefully and intentionally in the receiving space that Pastor Martha Postlethwaite describes in her poem "Clearing."

Wait there
patiently,
until the song
that is your life
falls into your own cupped hands.

At this time two years ago, I was sitting with my dad as the hospice chaplain read him the Sacrament of the Sick. Dad had been inwardly focused for weeks, mostly nonverbal with his eyes closed against the noise, confusion, and distraction of the outside world. The day that the hospice chaplain came, Dad was wide awake and eager to engage. I was so glad to look into his eyes and to share words of comfort, hugs, tears, and laughter. It seemed we were both surprised and delighted by the chance to connect. We spoke eagerly in sentence fragments and asked questions that didn't really need answers. As I described in *Without a Map*,

It felt as though Dad had come back from a deep and private place in order to say good-bye. I was so glad to be there and to be ready for the conversation he had wanted to have. I drove away wishing I had offered more or different words and that I had understood more of the meaning in his words. But I also drove away with a much lighter heart that afternoon and felt that Dad's heart was lightened too.

The comfort and connection of that day ushered us both into a peace that had been elusive for months. We were standing in the clearing, trusting what was to come.

It would be a month before he died. There were plenty of ups and downs yet to come, but at the time I was not thinking of the future or the past. I was simply grateful for this momentary deep breath of awareness and ease.

So much grace, learning, and vibrancy have fallen into my cupped hands since Dad died. I am honored by the gifts of insight and experience that I received in our journey together and I am so grateful for the opportunity to share our story with others now.

In the clearing, there is room enough for grief and gratitude. There is time for both joy and sorrow, laughter and tears. There is permission to know and permission not to know. There is peace.

And, in my cupped hands, there is room for it all.

And there is room left to wonder—about me, about you, about where we are and where we are going, and about what you find falling into your cupped hands.

Solstice Sunrise

For over a year, I have been watching sunrises. Waking in the quiet darkness, I move to the living room windows and watch the eastern sky. Most mornings, I do yoga as I keep watch out the window. Other mornings, I simply sit in peace and presence. I miss a few sunrises here and there when sleep is too sweet to interrupt or the nest inside the blankets is too warm to leave. On those days, I miss more than the sunrise. With the dawn, I set an intention to guide my words, actions, and thoughts for the day. At this time, whether in yoga or in meditation or both, my body, mind, and heart rise to greet the day. My daily intention emerges like the sun, slowly and reliably from behind the veil of night, sometimes a surprise but always a gift.

As the winter solstice approaches this year, I begin writing down my intentions. I think that subconsciously I am hoping to hold the gifts of the sunrise a bit longer as each day gets shorter. Alas, each morning I still seem to have to learn anew that the beauty of the sunrise doesn't linger. It is leaving even as it arrives. Impermanence resists holding. Impermanence is inevitable, and there is beauty in that too.

With this sunrise, I hold both the gifts and the challenges lightly, as the branches receive, hold, and release the new snow.

With this sunrise, emptiness sits heavily next to the fullness. Today I will hold them both gently.

With this sunrise, heavy clouds linger above the tree silhouettes. I am reminded that the universe is a continuum, darkness and light are one and the same.

With this sunrise, my heart opens fully to give and receive abundant love.

With this sunrise, I welcome each new moment as it arises.

With this sunrise, the woodstove springs to life, a beacon to the coming light outside the window.

With this sunrise, I welcome the gifts of love and family that surround me.

Winter Solstice

With the winter solstice approaching, the darkness seems to grow heavier. I vacillate between allowing myself to sink into it deeply and training my eyes to the light. Paying attention to the sunrise and the moonlight, I am reassured by the constancy and the flow of the light within the darkness. It takes courage to rise in the darkness each day. But each morning, as I am there to witness the sun nudging over the horizon, my courage grows.

I have always had a tricky relationship with winter. When the short days and long nights nudge me into bed early, I can get a little resentful. I know that I will eventually love the extra time for reflection and gentle appreciation that winter offers, but it can be hard to slow down. It feels like it takes me a little longer than the rest of the natural world to make the transition.

This year, as the solstice nears, I am grateful for the invitation to slow down and tune in to the comforts of the season. I pour my coffee and pull on a thick sweater before wrapping myself in a blanket in front of the woodstove. I am nurturing myself with slow, still warmth and light. But it is not just physical. I feel wrapped in a remembrance and an honoring that feel full, reverent, and nurturing.

The weeks between Thanksgiving and New Year's hold the anniversaries of the deaths of my father, grandfather, grandmother, and a family friend. These anniversaries are more than just notations on the calendar, they are memories of love and reflections of loss that come to me in waves of tender remembrance. As I hold my memories out in the light and really savor them, the intellectual memories of those who have died become distilled in body memories of our relationships. I hear and feel my father's love, my grandmother's delight, my grandfather's steadiness, and our friend's laughter. Though these individuals are no longer living, their presence is woven into mine to warm and illuminate this winter season. Beyond boundaries of time and space, beyond life and death, we remain together.

Barren Branches of Oak and Maple

Reaching to the sky like old and crooked fingers.
Swollen with time and age, bent in angles and curves,
Holding memories and experiences of days passed long ago.

Youthful flexibility tempered by challenges and growth,
Developing a rigidity accumulated from season to season.

Reaching upward and outward,
Beckoning to the sun and moon alike
In honor to each passing day.

Reaching upward and outward,
Calling me to pay attention.
Notice the sky.
See the beauty in these twisted tendrils.
Celebrate the youth that has passed
And the age that has arrived.
Live this day.

Empty deciduous branches of winter,
Hold nothing but the weight of the sky,
The love of those crooked fingers,
Remembrance of yesterday,
And the joy of today.

Blessings All

Years ago, I found a little slip of paper while I was cleaning out my desk. I recognized it as a note included with the homemade calendar that my grandfather sent every year around Thanksgiving. This calendar included the birthdays and anniversaries of my grandparents' children and their spouses, their grandchildren and their spouses, and all of the great-grandchildren born to date. Despite long distances, philosophical differences, and ordinary family dysfunction, the calendar tethered fifty people and one hundred years of lives and relationships. Each year when I received it, I was reminded that my grandparents provided a centripetal focus for all of our orbits. Through them, we each remained in some form of relationship with one another, vitally connected to both our ancestry and our legacy.

Blessings All.
Our memory of the past defines our hope for the future.

Something about the note must have resonated with me at the time, because I tucked it in a drawer to be discovered and considered another day. When it emerged during my desk cleaning, Dad was rapidly declining with dementia. At the time, we were working hard to hold together the pieces of a life that was determined to unravel. Despite our attentive and creative efforts, his world continued to become more and more unfamiliar and confusing every day. On some days, the note seemed to taunt me, demanding that I figure out how to retain enough memories—for me and for Dad—that we could both find hope in this very hopeless situation. On other days, the message simply seemed misguided. Dad did not have memories to rely on at all and did not seem to forecast toward the future. I noticed, though, that he fully lived the present moments that arrived throughout each day. Each new moment was greeted with openness and curiosity. Because he had been released from expectation, a certain freedom had emerged. I learned to follow his lead and soon found myself somewhat released from the past and future too.

Our memory of the past defines our hope for the future.

Eventually I reconciled with the note. Memory of the past and hope for the future can be important tethers, like the calendar. They connect us to an ancient future and a distant past that keep us grounded in awareness and responsibility. They hold us in relationship with the rest of creation over all time and place and remind us that we are a part of the whole. But neither memory nor hope can shape our relationships or our actions. Those are best tended in each moment.

Blessings All.

The slip of paper still sits on my desk where I can see it often. It still makes me think of my grandfather and his calendars. It also makes me think of Dad and the love and good living that we shared when we released the past and future and, instead, walked purposefully into each present moment. It reminds me to appreciate both memory and hope while also giving my care and attention to inhabiting each moment.

The note no longer teases or frustrates me. It strengthens my resolve to contribute to healing and wholeness. It focuses my attention on the world that my children are inheriting. Their hope for the future is in the words and actions of the young people and adults around them who speak and act with compassion for others and for the living earth. Their hope hinges on what we do today. Today I will honor each arising moment with an open heart, a clear mind, honest words and actions, and good intentions.

Winter Compost

I have always thought that we compost year-round at our house. We use two closed bins to avoid attracting critters to our backyard and our chickens. The bins work on an annual rotation—we add our compost to one bin at a time while the other "rests."

This resting bin is a fertile cavern of activity. Inside, microbes, worms, and fungi change the apple cores, eggshells, and other food waste into dark, nutrient-rich soil. By the end of the summer, our discards are ready to become the foundation for next season's garden. Every fall, we put one of our garden beds to bed with the fully cooked compost from the resting bin.

Once empty, the bin is ready for contributions. This winter, I am watching the bin fill as the compost pile inside grows taller and taller; I realize that we are freezing rather than composting. The last few times that I have brought out the compost, I have wondered how much more I will be able to fit into the bin. We have never run out of space before. I don't ever recall having a frozen pile of banana peels, carrot tops, and withered greens rising to meet me when I take off the lid. What have we done differently this year to create a food scrap stalagmite rather than a decaying pile of organic matter?

In previous years, maybe there was enough organic matter left in the bin to begin and maintain a modest rate of decomposition throughout the winter. Or maybe the deep freeze of early January killed or stunned the microscopic beings that are responsible for sustaining the transformation from scrap to soil. Or maybe we are eating a greater volume of fruits and vegetables that have skins, cores, seeds, and stalks that are bound for the compost. Whatever the reason, we are freezing rather than composting this winter. The growing pile of perfectly intact food scraps is a little absurd, but I continue to contribute to it.

Every bucket added to the pile feels like an act of affirmation that the cycle will continue. I have observed the interplay and repeated cycling between decomposition and creation dozens of times in the garden and forest. This year, in the frozen pile of food scraps, the cycle has slowed, perhaps even suspended for the winter season. The compost's long pause is a good reminder to find time, space, and safety to rest and reflect amid the activities of our days and years.

In our journey from birth to death, we have thousands, maybe millions, of opportunities to create, break down, cycle, and recycle. Between each opportunity, there is an opportunity for a moment of stillness. In each of these moments, we can take note of the process that brought us to it and wonder about the one that will follow. Sometimes glaringly obvious and sometimes barely perceptible, the pause is an integral part of the cycle too. It exists in the subtle time and space between inhale and exhale, between dawn and day, between speaking and silence. It exists in a time and space that is both hollow and full beyond measure. The pause is fleeting and slippery, but I know it when I have moved through it. In this year of all time and no time, the pause visits often and I am learning to harvest its gifts.

No matter how long or short, every still moment eventually yields to motion. At the compost pile, spring will come. With the warmth and movement, the compost pile and garden will "spring to life" in a flurry of decay and decomposition, beauty and growth. I will be looking for the subtle pauses that coexist within the cycles. They are there, too.

While I tend the garden, I will also be settling more deeply into the pauses of my daily life by regularly practicing stillness and reflection. I will create more spaciousness by stepping out of routines that restrict time and energy. I will value the solitary space and time that slows my pace and hones my intentions. I will live deeply into the sacred pauses that pepper my days.

And I will turn the compost and weed the carrots, taking my place in the cycles of dissolution and creation that will always surround the sacred pause.

Imbolc

Imbolc, the midwinter observance between the winter solstice and the spring equinox, arrives when the land is covered in deep snow. Under this thick blanket, the seeds buried deep underground sense a shift. Aboveground, critters of all types stir. I too feel the restless energy. This is known as the quickening. Nights are long and cold; days are short and crisp. But the sun is rising earlier each day and setting a little later. Daily, the earth receives this ever-increasing light at a more direct angle. These are the days when it is possible to ski or snowshoe for hours, warmed by bright sun on my face and my own effort. The snow is soft and deep; the air is cold but no longer bites. The promise of spring lingers close by, but there is no mistaking the fact that the world remains deeply frozen.

The long, dark winter nights begin to give way to longer days. The sun rises higher in the sky. At Imbolc, the stirring and the restlessness can tempt us into motion, but it is important not to jump too soon. A seed planted before the soil is warm enough will rot in the ground. An idea birthed before its time will struggle to find footing. When Imbolc pulls you from your deep winter slumber, feed the fire and sit for a moment to gaze at the moon and stars. Winter is not done yet.

Imbolc seems to invite me to notice the incoming spring and

make preparations. Some days that preparation is planning for work that lies ahead. Other days it is rest in anticipation of the labor ahead. Imbolc marks a season of deep reflection and growing awareness. Resting too fully in either is incomplete. Holding both the weighty darkness and the growing light expands our capacity to carry and honor the fullness of our lives, the depths and the heights, the sorrows and the joys.

The light is returning, and its subtle nudges poke and prod. Every once in a while, I see glimmers of the possibility, but some days I am here, in the compost pile. The decomposition is rapid. I am decomposing, breaking down the aspects of my life into enough little bits that they can be repurposed. The integrity of each particular scenario is still here. Some experiences resemble the banana peel; it takes longer to decompose into nutrients that can be accessed by the living ecosystem around it. Likewise, some of my memories retain their hardened edges. They refuse to yield and offer their rich nutrients of lessons and values to the wider landscape of my experience. Time will work on them slowly and surely. Meanwhile, I have other fodder for growing. Some experiences have long ago become rich, loamy soil, worked and reworked until only dreamlike lessons in love and life remain. Others have more recently broken down into usable components. My connection to spirit remains nascent. But rather than decomposing matter, it feels like microbes in the system. This connection to spirit is akin to the connective fungal threads that travel through the soil. They offer unity by connecting the decomposing elements. The connection to spirit is the thread that has been here all along.

Midwinter

This morning, as every morning, I take our dog, Karma, for a walk just a few minutes before it is time to warm up the car for the drive to school. I am often tempted to abbreviate this walk, urged along by the cold air on my face and the sense of urgency that can accompany the last fifteen minutes before departure. Today, however, I am glad to walk the whole loop. Something needs to be explored. Karma feels it too, pausing longer than usual to smell clumps of grass peeking out of the snowy patches. Coyotes, foxes, deer, and turkeys often come through the field, but the snow is so crusty and icy right now they don't leave footprints. Without the footprints, I don't see evidence of their passing, but they leave behind a scent for Karma to discover. In one spot, she catches the scent of something buried below the icy snow. She stops to scratch and sniff. Not finding it, she scratches and sniffs again, and again. She makes it through the snow and to the dirt, but whatever she smells remains elusive. Something enticing is there, just beyond her nose and invisible to me, but it is clearly there.

Later in the morning, I gather with a group of people to celebrate Imbolc. I think of Karma as we acknowledge the quickening, the returning light. The growing light awakens a subtle energy in all living beings. It had definitely stirred Karma, and I sense it in myself as well. The lengthening days invite inspiration and the crisp, cold air invigorates; the dark, cold nights nurture the dormancy that births creativity. I sense it in the earth. Can we sense it in one another? Most importantly, can we give ourselves over to it and live into it even more fully?

Imbolc's invitation to become aware of my own seasonal awakening feels like an invitation to affirm the natural rhythms of my life. I often experience my cycles of energy and fatigue as products of my life and only occasionally remember that they also flow naturally with rhythms of days, seasons, and years. This morning, I realize that stepping into those rhythms with greater intention honors my wholehearted, whole-bodied participation in the cycle of life. I want to dwell more fully in that participation.

The Buddha's life followed a very deliberate pattern of withdrawal and return. As Huston Smith describes in *The World's Religions*, "The Buddha withdrew for six years, then returned for forty-five years. But each year was likewise divided: nine months in the world, followed by a three-month retreat with his monks during the rainy season. His daily cycle, too, was patterned to this mold. His public hours were long, but three times a day, he withdrew, to return his attention (through meditation) to its sacred source."

This apparent seesaw between withdrawal and return (rest and exertion, struggle and acceptance) creates a delicate balance. A harmony is achieved by making intentional space for both the effort and the retreat. This feels like a true and heartening counterbalance to the cultural message to continuously achieve, produce, and consume. While I would not attempt to emulate the Buddha's life practice specifically, it offers an aspirational example. Karma was also leading by example earlier this morning. The hardy souls who joined me later to nourish our spirits with a celebration and a walk in the woods were also showing the way.

There is balance in the dance between light and shadow, giving and receiving, waking and sleeping. At this midwinter, I will embrace the always-shifting cycles within and around me with renewed gratitude and appreciation for both the waxing and the waning. And, whether the groundhog sees his shadow or not tomorrow, I will be paying attention to the stirrings of the new day.

Holding On and Letting Go

As I approach the woods, a gentle wind stirs the air. Snowballs, crystals, fairy dust, and wonder rise from the tree branches before lightly and playfully falling to the ground. The field is covered in a full, fresh layer of snow. It looks like winter, but the temperature of the air and the depth of blue in the sky hint toward spring. This snow is not destined to last long. It is late winter, and the season is more fickle than ever.

The pines and maples surrounding the field at the edge of the forest hold piles of heavy snow. Some of the trees hold the fresh

snow as if in a gentle hug, happy for the temporary companionship. Others seem burdened by the uninvited guest, sagging
under the new weight. The oak trees, which also still hold many
of their leaves from the previous fall, seem especially laden. With
each gust, though, each tree releases a little more snow. As the
wind whispers through the branches, I hear an audible sigh of
relief as the trees release their loads.

I sit for a while with the little oak at the top of the drainage. I
feel some kinship with this tree and its long, reaching branches. It
will hold on to the leaves of the last growing season until emerging buds push them off in the spring. This oak, nestled out of the
wind, will also hold the day's snow longer than most of its neighbors. There does not appear to be any burden in this holding.
This little tree seems designed to hold on. Its trunk is straight and
solid. The branches grow low and wide. The fibers of each branch
are dense. It clings to last season, embraces the snow of this season, and prepares for the growth of spring and summer ahead.
This little tree declares that it is possible to have and hold it all.

Like the oak, I too attempt to hold—or at least juggle—it all.
There is joy in this rich fullness. It can also be stifling and inhib-
iting. Dwelling on the regrets, mistakes, and successes of the past
does not leave space for recognizing the gifts of today. Attending
to the longing, anticipation, or worry for the future does not
allow for living into the potential of each moment. When I am
holding too much or too tightly, the present passes without notice
and intent.

Holding on can also be comforting, serving us well from time
to time. I remember helping Dad pack up his condo when he was
moving to a residential care facility in Maine. I picked up a candy
dish that I had never seen before and asked him if he wanted to
take it with him. He looked at it for a long time while I watched
him drift far into his thoughts. Finally, he returned and said, "Yes,
let's take that. It reminds me of my grandmother." We packed it
up, and it stayed by his bedside for the next three years. Dad had
lost so much to dementia and would lose so much more. Holding

on to that dish and any memories that it carried was a small and tender grace.

Now, when I see that dish in my house, it reminds me of Dad. Specifically, it reminds me of holding him close and offering care during the years of his decline. And it reminds me of the paradox that was so strong at his death. After days by his bedside, I finally felt myself letting go of his barely living body. As I did, I remembered that I had felt the power of his spirit releasing into the world several days before he died. Noticing that I had been clinging to physical life, and being intentional about letting it go, allowed my awareness of his persistent and expanding essence to return.

I see similar expansion in my boys as they explore the world and create their spaces within it. Now teenagers, they are taking longer, more independent steps into those spaces. Much of it happens out of my sight, but the growing strength and freedom feels very similar to the days when they were just learning to walk or climb trees. It was important to stay close at first, but as strength and confidence grew, it was important to step farther and farther away. They needed to know that they were capable and that I trusted in their power and ability. They also needed to know that I was nearby if they wanted or needed me. Letting go is not the same as walking away. Letting go is an opening of hugging arms. Letting go honors both past and potential while holding space for the present.

By now, the little oak in the drainage is beginning to release her snow. As the sun rises higher, the snow melts away one slow drip at a time. As I walk away from the tree, I begin to walk a spiral in the middle of the field. Both the lithe trees at the edge of the field and the stiff, stoic oak at the top of the drainage had offered a rich teaching. There are times for holding on, and there are times for letting go.

As I wrap into the spiral, I feel how closely connected the two actions are. Sometimes we are walking into the center, contracting, focusing, and holding. At other times, we are walking out toward the edges, expanding, stretching, and letting go. Holding on and letting go are expressions of love on the same continuum. The dance between them becomes the way that we nurture ourselves and our relationships, and the way that we live our lives.

Today, I am letting go. The struggles and sorrows of our human family and ailing planet often hang heavily on my heart, and I hold them closely. But today, the snow and sun are calling for company and I will stay out to play.

Salve of Hope and Healing

Fog closes in as the warm air mingles with the coolness of the rapidly melting snow. This is spring, or a step toward it, anyhow. There will still be steps back into winter. This is how seasonal change comes. Two steps forward and one step backward. Indeed, perhaps this is how most change comes—in fits and starts, the result of slow, plodding steps in one particular direction. Periodically, we try to step back for reassurance that the past has not dissolved before we have found a solid future to stand on. An occasional detour takes us around obstacles, but motion continues. This is how we age, reliably and subtly. This is how friendships develop or dissolve, slowly and steadily. This is how winter gives way to spring, inevitably. While this also seems to be how topsoil erodes from fields, forests shrink, species go extinct, oceans warm, and our cultural and economic superiority contests result in unimaginable human and ecological devastation, I cannot accept those changes as inevitable. The daily continuation and escalation of shortsighted policies and practices brings us to horrific realities that we have learned, for better or worse, to live alongside.

I ingest world news in very small and measured doses. I am too easily overwhelmed by the scale and persistence of the world's suffering and the decisions that perpetuate it. So when news does come across my radar screen, I know that I am meant to pay attention to it. This morning, I read about an airstrike on a neighborhood hospital in Yemen. The U.S.-supported war in Yemen is not *new* news, but the latest report hits me especially hard. I do not justify or condone any act of war, but I am particularly stunned and saddened by the depravity of targeting a hospital.

Detours, aging, and friendships seem integral and inevitable to the progression of the human experience. I do not accept warplanes and civilian airstrikes as essential to that arc—yet here we are. And I do not accept the greed, fear, and resentments that have arisen slowly and surely to a point where wars of all sizes smolder in homes, villages, and cities across this beautiful planet. People are hurting each other, killing each other. Surely human conflict has existed for as long as there have been humans, but the tools we currently have for inflicting damage are diverse and devastating. I cannot settle in this reality.

I find myself wanting to walk quickly through this stage of human existence, into a different reality. Actually, walking is not enough; I want to run, to get to the other side as fast as possible. But really, running feels more like running away than running through. And I can't turn away from it. The hurt of the human heart did not grow in a day; it will not resolve in a day. This hurt calls me to hold it tenderly and fiercely, wrapped in the arms of hope. The suffering and the solution are within me and in everything that I put out into the world.

So I will hold and honor the suffering as a necessary part of the healing. I will continue to walk toward a different future, surely and confidently. I will offer words and actions that reflect the love and light underlying the human spirit, the Universal Spirit. I will transmute the greed and fear that grip me by leaning into forgiveness, love, and compassion. I will live it in my daily life and work with others to cultivate it in our educational, political, and corporate structures. I am sure we can develop a social mindset that welcomes and embraces the human spirit. Beneath the greatest acts of heroism and the worst acts of terror resides the same potential for love and goodness. When we embrace the humanity—the divinity—that resides within each of us, it feels possible that we will begin to unlock the potential to heal our relationships with one another and with the planet.

There is a kind of change that happens so fast you don't see it coming—and sometimes you hardly remember what it replaced. This is the change of snowstorms that cover the field overnight. This is the change of an empty house crumbling and the corner store closing. This is the change held in the crocus that emerges, seemingly out of nowhere, in the warmth of a morning. This is the change of people rising everywhere to recognize the common humanity in every other person with whom they share their time on Earth. This is the rapid change that will come when enough people realize that *we are the ones* we've been waiting for.

> Rising with the sun,
> I too offer light and heat.
> Gifts of love,
> Salve of hope and healing,
> Nourishment for our hurting planet.

Spring Equinox

Each spring, I am startled by new insight and energy for the work that lies ahead in the growing season. My own experience of spring rests upon centuries of human experience of the same turning season. My experience of new insight and energy, therefore, fuses with that of all the other human and more-than-human beings who are experiencing the same increasing light and warmth. As we merge with the generations that came before, we experience a profound relief and renewed energy as winter's grip releases. This union of my finite, lived experience with the eternal world invigorates and inspires me. But my anticipation and eager energy to participate in the cycle can be exhausting.

The warm, sunlit Quaker meeting house that I attend is a wonderful place to be reminded regularly to slow my pace and quiet my thoughts. During "waiting worship" we listen for the small, still voice within ourselves—that is, the voice of the divine that is speaking through us. In a posture of waiting that is neither expectant nor anxious, I cultivate a receptivity to the mysteries of the world around me. I regain a capacity to hold the extremes, remembering that the deep sleep of winter and the wakefulness of summer are balanced by these midpoints. I remember that when we hold space for the darkness and the light, the warmth and the cold, there is ample room. In the expansive silence of waiting worship, both everything and nothing are equally welcome.

Each spring, as the asparagus emerges in the garden, I am surprised, grateful, and humbled. I watch for it, but I do not yearn for it. Checking the surface of the soil daily for signs of movement is waiting worship in the garden. Like the spoken messages that arrive during worship, it is nothing short of a miracle when this green, nutrient-filled plant emerges from the just-thawed earth. It follows its own timeline, a timeline that is closely connected to the increasing sunlight and warmth. In the last few years, the first shoots have arrived as early as April and as late as May. When they arrive, I know the other garden beds are ready to be planted. And I know we will have asparagus for breakfast and dinner for the next four to six weeks while we wait for the other vegetables to establish. Most importantly, I am reminded that there is a life-affirming, life-sustaining rhythm that is supporting me always.

Waxing Moon, Melting Snow

Last night, as I stood under the stars, the waxing crescent moon caught my eye. Over the next ten days, its light will steadily grow until it is high in the sky, illuminating the midnight field as if it were twilight. I imagine the snow and ice will continue their slow and steady melt during that same time.

The signs of spring are clear. The eaves of the roof are dripping steadily. In the morning, the smell of the skunk who passed by in the night lingers and the early birds persistently declare their presence. The critters are stirring. It is no wonder that I am stirring too.

I am a lover of light. My body is fully aware that we are nearing the spring equinox. The current cycle of the moon amplifies that recognition. Longer, brighter, warmer days infuse my body with energy, my mind with creativity, and my heart with gratitude. Bright moonlit nights encourage me to linger on my evening walk.

While the light is growing, the darkness is receding. There is a gentle gestation that can only happen under the shroud of darkness and the deep, contemplative hibernation of winter. It is hard to simply let go of the safety and comfort of the dark cave that has held and nurtured me through the previous long months. But when I honor it and give thanks for it, I can hold both the shrinking, dark coolness and the expanding, bright warmth with equal appreciation.

I am reminded to remain present. There is abundant beauty, love, and learning in each moment. I feel them deeply when I attend to the reality that each moment contains the delicate balance between light and dark, expansion and contraction. The present moment is the only time and place to experience the fullness of life's offering.

Easter Peepers

The peepers are here! Some people get excited about the appearance of Peeps, the brightly colored sugar-coated marshmallow confections that also show up around this time. But I am delighted by the spring peepers.

In the patch of field and forest where we live, the high-pitched call of these petite woodland frogs fills the air at dusk in the early spring. The chorus can be so loud that it feels like there must be thousands of them, each trying to call the loudest to attract a mate and establish territory. After a long winter and a tentative early spring, their boisterous presence assures me that we have really entered the season of growth, fecundity, and abundance. The peepers are singing before the crocuses have even poked out of the ground!

Each year when the peepers begin calling, I am reminded of a fatal mistake we made a number of years ago. The boys were very young and endlessly curious about the critters that live in our forest. We had been maintaining a rotating aquarium of sorts for a few months, collecting bugs, frogs, or salamanders from our creek and bringing them inside to observe for a few days. We always took them back, hoping to let them go before captivity had caused too much stress. Releasing them where we had found them, we thanked them for allowing us to study them. We were trying to be careful, reverent amateur naturalists. Our collection, maintenance, and release were guided by the principle that we would do no harm.

One summer day, we found a big blob of frog eggs in a water-filled depression in the field. For several days, we eagerly went back to check on them, hoping to observe metamorphosis. We didn't see any changes in the eggs, but we did notice that their habitat was drying up. We worried that maybe the frog had chosen her nursery poorly and that there might not be enough water to sustain the eggs long enough for the coming transformations to tadpole and frog. Just before the puddle went dry, we decided to help.

We put fresh water from the creek and the egg mass into our aquarium. Over the course of a few days, rather than observing frog metamorphosis, we watched the mass of eggs dissolve into a blob of gelatinous goop. We hadn't helped at all. Maybe we had even harmed. Maybe the eggs of this species would not begin to transform until they began to dry. With regret, we took the goop and water outside and gave them back to the earth. The boys seemed to absorb the loss, but I was distressed by our "help" gone wrong. It still rattles me. We had the best intentions, but we had catastrophically interrupted the natural life cycle of a being with whom we share this land.

Every spring, I wait anxiously for the peepers to begin their chorus. For a few years, they seemed substantially quieter. I attributed the muffled sound to population loss, a loss likely caused by human intrusion, including ours. I know it is irrational to think that we wiped out a whole region of the species with our egg collection that year, but reason doesn't have a lot of influence when there's guilt involved. Recently, I have learned that spring peepers lay their eggs singly, rather than in masses, and they hatch in a few days. The mass we collected (and killed) belonged to a different species. I do not know its name, its habits, or its call. I can only hope that it is flourishing today.

This wet spring seems to be good for the peepers. They are loud this year, and their strong presence is good for me. My heart seems to join them in song each evening. In the morning, I watch the puddles, depressions, and ponds for egg masses. If I find any, I will watch them and wish them well—but I will not interfere.

I can best serve the earth as a witness and participant in the enduring cycle of life. And I can best serve this cycle as an advocate for human systems, both large and small, that will recognize, honor, and protect it too. I will honor birth, death, and transformation in my life and in all life, fully embracing the eternal cycles of creation. What more could an amateur naturalist hope for?

Small, Still Voice

In Quaker tradition, "centering down" refers to the process of quieting the body and mind in order to attend to the small, still voice that resides within us. That voice is our conscience, our moral compass—that of God within us, spirit expressed through us. Whatever identity we assign it, that voice is the conduit through which the divine is expressed in our common lives. I think of it as the voice of my true self. Centering down requires getting comfortable enough sitting quietly that the internal chatter of our daily lives is replaced by "expectant waiting" for expression of the spirit.

Truth be told, I find it really hard to center down through silence and stillness. I can, however, find my small, still voice when I am in motion. I figured this out in high school while running long miles to "clear my head" on the weekends. After about thirty minutes of trotting down the road, I would pass a threshold that I always thought of as the "cotton-candy line." With my mind enmeshed in soft, fluffy sweetness, my self-conscious deliberations of daily life would dissolve and leave space for clearer and more creative exploration of problems and their solutions. In this open space, while still running, I could finish my homework, solve social problems, and reflect on potential from a place that had clearly originated beyond my conscious thought. I always assumed that this was a result of some hormonal or chemical response that opened neural pathways that would remain closed in the absence of focused exertion. I now realize that it was just my way of centering down.

Since high school, I have channeled that compulsion for motion into running, walking, hiking, trail work, and gardening. I have conceived many written pages, designed and led youth programs, and built my strongest and deepest relationships while moving. The motion has provided both the catalyst and the foundation for my life's best work.

In *The Book of Joy*, Archbishop Desmond Tutu describes his daily constitutional as meditation in motion, a pathway for accessing the wisdom of the spirit that comes through the wisdom of the body. I think of this as a wisdom of the heart, and it sustains and informs me well beyond the exercise itself. If I jump right into the obligations of a day without taking time for my physically engaged version of centering down, I spend the day reacting to situations and information around me. I am anxious rather than accepting when I notice that I will be late for an appointment. I am quick to anger or sadness when I hear accounts of hate and bigotry rather than feeling the compassion that has the potential to transform the negative thoughts and energy. These days it feels ever more important to make sure that I am able to speak and act from a place of peace and compassion, which can only come from within.

My teenage boys are increasingly engaged in the world outside our family and close friends. They consume media reports of global events with the same zeal that they consume large quantities of food. They work to reconcile headlines with their emerging beliefs about the world and the people of the world. The violent and mean-spirited words and actions at play on the national and

international stage are inconsistent with the acceptance, toler-
ance, and awareness they have practiced in their short lives. As
I try to buffer their absorption of this ugliness, my thoughts get
tangled up in disbelief and resentment. I shouldn't have to try to
explain intolerance, hatred, racism, and bigotry. These behaviors
and beliefs don't hold up to attempts at rational explanation. My
mind cannot make any meaning from this madness. Instead, I
rely on sharing the wisdom of my heart.

I have always ascribed more value to the wisdom of the heart
than the efforts of the mind. Lately, I start most days with a walk
or a yoga practice in order to open the pathways to the thoughts
and feelings that come from deep within. Beginning the day in
motion, I have a chance to sink deeply into my own body, listening for the small, still voice within me and setting my intentions
for the day. From this place, I have the best chance of holding on
to my authentic motivations as the external demands and inputs
of contemporary life pull me into reflexive responses. Tapped into
my internal energy rather than swept up in the frenetic energy
of the world around me, I am more likely to be the person that I
wish to be for my children, my community, and the wider world.

My small, still voice advocates clearly for love, compassion,
and acceptance. It doesn't leave room for anything else. Still, I
need to refresh my connection to it throughout the day—and
that is best done outside. A few minutes walking along the trail,
working in the garden, chopping wood, or shoveling snow clarifies my voice. The words and actions that come from that heart
wisdom are amplified when I have spent even a few minutes in
motion under a wide and welcoming sky or a protective canopy
of trees. Reconnecting, even briefly, with the rhythms of my body
and the rhythms of the natural world refreshes my capacity to
hear and abide by the wisdom of my heart. These moments of
meditation in motion sprinkled throughout the day invite me to
center down again and again.

Beltane

Summer has arrived. The spring transition can be cool and rainy, so the warmer days that are arriving now truly feel like summer. The days are getting long. It is still light when I go to bed and dark when I wake up. At Beltane (a.k.a. May Day), we celebrate the earth's increasing energy and the beginning of the growing season. I, too, celebrate my own growing energy.

The singing birds are less persistent and less urgent now. They seem now to sing for the joy of being here, not for the search. Perhaps having found the mate, home, and nourishment that will fulfill their season, they sing for the pleasure of the singing. Perhaps, though, it is all really for the pleasure of the singing. Like the birds, I feel the urgency to be of use, to manifest my potential. I must, as the Indigenous attorney, activist, and teacher Sherri Mitchell describes in her book *Sacred Instructions*, live out the sacred instructions that I was born with.

In other words, I am compelled to do the work that only I am able to manifest in this world at this time. I recognize that I am here for a reason. That both motivates and humbles me. If I allow myself to sink into the self-doubt—*What is it I am supposed to do? Am I capable?*—it can be paralyzing. But when I accept that I have all that I need to live my potential, I am encouraged. I move forward with confidence—one foot in front of the other, following a path that my heart recognizes. My eyes may not be able to see it, my mind may not understand how or why, but my heart has wisdom that I trust. My heart understands the sacred instructions and follows the labyrinth of their unfolding. I must avoid being impatient or persistent or trying to see beyond what is here, now. When I keep at bay the cultural training that requires empirical understanding, I understand wholly. My being reverberates with the energy of this living earth. I feel its pain and trust its capacity for healing. I recognize its beauty, and I see its harshness.

I, too, embody these balancing opposites. I, too, am at a tipping point. The seed containing my sacred instructions has cracked open. The potential that has been quietly waiting for this time is beginning to open into itself. I am ready. I am here.

Blossoms

Earlier this week, I was watching blossoms unfurl on the plum tree. I checked the tight green buds eagerly each day, anticipating the grand display of flowers to come. Slowly, they began to open. But instead of a grand display, it has been a gradual unveiling. Each blossom is an individual with a time frame of its own, a potential that will unfold at the right time, no sooner, no later.

I notice how, like the blossoms, I am unfolding very slowly to this season, risking exposure only in bits. Perhaps the plum tree's rhythm protects the harvest from early frost that could damage the earliest bloomers. What is my caution protecting me from? I quietly nurtured projects and inspirations through the winter; spring would be the right time for them to explode onto the scene with color and vibrancy. The symbolism is inviting, but the reality is much more complicated. Opening too much heart or imagination too quickly feels risky. There is so much potential in front of me, and each opportunity promises (or threatens) to open more doors. How much can I take on, and how far out can I step?

This is not really a question I need to answer intellectually.

My body offers all of the answers. At times, it offers energy and inspiration; that's when I work and play. At other times, I am completely depleted, unable to act against the lethargy in my body or mind; that is when I slow down, take stock, and sleep longer. Paying attention to these natural inclinations to work, play, and rest, I can see that my cycle of opening into this new season is disciplined and steady, like that of the plum tree. That observation, the sense of kinship, sparks new patience for my pace. It kindles a compassionate reminder to let go of my waiting and urgency and to simply pay attention to what is real and present in each moment, both within and around me.

Today, the plum tree is in full bloom. Each individual blossom has opened, and the flowers' collective beauty is jaw-dropping. Dozens of bees are collecting and sharing pollen from flower to flower, branch to branch, tree to tree. There will be fruit this year—and it will come in due time.

Winds of Change

A few nights ago, a strong breeze blew through. It was pushing out a cool, soggy day and ushering in a warm, sunny evening. As I stood in the orchard watching the leaves wave and the branches bend, I couldn't help wondering what else it might be ushering in or out. It felt capable of the strong magic that could blow in Mary Poppins or transform the Kansas of our present times to the Oz of the near future. As I felt the wind on my face and in my hair, I daydreamed and wondered.

Is this the sudden shift of energy that will usher in harmony and balance to humanity?

Could the earth help blow away the ills of our society and blow in its health?

Is there someone nearby experiencing a significant shift?

Standing in the wind, I was reminded of the breeze that blew the day before Thatcher was born. There was no doubt in my mind that it was ushering in new life. The convergence of energy and air outside had something to do with the life force that was in my body, preparing to make an entrance into the world. With my contractions slowly growing, I walked aimlessly through the neighborhood. The cool air on my cheeks and the swirling dandelion seeds were reassuring mirrors of the powerful energy that was building in me. The intensity of the wind and the alternating dark clouds and bright blue sky held both dark and light, ferocity and safety. As I observed the interplay of these external forces, I was acutely aware that they were also at play inside my body. Moreover, they had a life of their own.

As I walked, I remembered the words of comfort and encouragement that my friend Su had spoken to me when I was in early labor with Duncan. I had called her in a panic, certain that I could not go through with this birth process. The intense emotions and contractions were too scary, too painful.

"I can't do it," I told her.

She listened patiently and then reassured me that I could. "The only way out is to go through to the other side." She was right, of course. I could do this: I was born for this. Emerging on the other side, I joined a long, proud lineage of awestruck first-time mothers when my son entered the world.

Two years later, remembering her wise words and reveling in the wind energy around me, I felt my individual autonomy disappear, replaced by a sense of being held by this collective lineage. I surrendered myself to the labor and power of the birthing process, trusting in the ancient, inherited wisdom carried in my female body. In the face of this powerful, shifting life-force energy, acceptance and openness were my only possible responses. The next morning, as the wind subsided and the sun began to rise, Thatcher was born with all the strength of that wind that blew him in. We welcomed him with love.

The wind continued to blow strong yesterday as the city

of Portland, Maine, prepared to meet the needs of hundreds of asylum seekers being transferred from the Texas border. Most of them had been traveling toward safety for many months. The new arrivals quickly overwhelmed the city's established shelter system, and an emergency shelter was set up in the Portland Expo with the expectation of offering safe temporary housing and food to up to 350 individuals in the next week. Individuals and organizations stepped forward to offer food, clothing, blankets, and legal and interpretive services. As a whole, the community responded swiftly and generously to welcome these people in need.

Reading the initial reports, I felt proud to be a Mainer. But I was also surprised to find disparaging comments about the generosity—panicky voices of fear responding to requests for assistance with "I can't," "I won't," and "It's not my responsibility," people grasping at the illusion of their control and separation even as cooperative action unfolded around them. I wished I could offer them the same assurance, comfort, and confidence that Su had offered me many years ago: The only way out of this is to go through to the other side. It isn't possible to opt out. There is new life being born, not just for the asylum seekers but for all of us. Humans are social creatures. We are meant to step in close with one another. In fact, we were born for this.

Sherri Mitchell describes these evolutionary times as "the long, dark birth canal, and the Great Mother is in the throes of her laboring pain." The analogy gets at the squeeze, fear, and promise of these times. There is a strong wind of change blowing. We respond by alternating between contraction and expansion, generating ever-greater energy. When we give ourselves to the possibility and promise inherent in this process, joining the light and energy within us to the shifting energy around us, we contribute to the emergence. On the other side of the long, dark birth canal is a new life full of love, possibility, and an energy of its own. On the other side of the dark, blustery night is a sunny, nurturing day. Shadow and light will always interplay, but we can choose to give our energy to the light. When we do, we may just find that the Mary Poppins magic has been here all along in the strong breezes, gentle wind, and still skies. It is here in our hearts.

May we greet each other with openness and acceptance.

May we welcome new life with love.

May the strong winds around us and within us usher in new life and possibility.

May we remember that we were born for this.

Mother's Day Marathon

As I drove to the beach yesterday, I found myself following the route of a running race in progress. Judging by the distance that I drove alongside the racers, I guessed it was a marathon. The runners and I were traveling in opposite directions, so I was able to observe faces and bodies. Their gaits and expressions held joy, struggle, effort, and perseverance. The runners came in all shapes, sizes, and levels of fitness, but they shared a common stance of determination. After passing hundreds of these running, jogging, walking, and stretching humans, I felt a wave of emotion. Tears began to form. I was witnessing human potential being realized.

Each of these individuals had set their sights on a goal, likely a stretch for many of them, and I was getting to watch their final reach for it. For most of them, race day was likely the culmination of months of training, which had included planning, hopes, sacrifices, disappointments, and successes. I know the routine; I used to run long distances. For me, the race was very important. It offered a goal, something to move toward, a reason to keep running even when I didn't feel like it. But the greatest value I gained from running was in the training, not the racing. During training, I learned to stretch my limits, find a reliable pace, and persist through discomfort or malaise. On race day—and every other day—these new skills gave me confidence, courage, and capacity for any opportunity that I pursued.

Watching these runners, I was reminded of the vast potential available to each of us. Humans are infinitely creative and capable. I suddenly imagined that the same determination and inspiration that allow humans to run marathons—and heal illnesses, solve problems, overcome addictions—will help us heal our relationships to one another and to the earth. I envisioned that when we turn our singular individual devotions to the collective need, we will begin to cultivate the peace that is possible. Some days, I believe it is already happening. Yesterday was one of those days.

When I arrived at the beach, I walked directly to the water's edge, where the receding tide was exposing more and more walkable beach each minute. Standing there, I gave thanks to the earth, mother of us all, for its boundless capacity to nurture my body and soul. Earlier this week, I had written a card to my mom, feeling gratitude for the gifts of life and love that she gives me. And then I had written a note to my oldest son, thanking him for turning me into a mama. Our possibilities and intentions are nurtured in many layers. Mothering unlocked my own potential for growing and loving, while also creating tangible hope for the future and tethering me, and our children, to our ancestral lineage. Mothering provides daily training for the work of nurturing the wider community that I feel called to do.

At a workshop I attended recently, Sherri Mitchell shared an interesting bit of biological fact: Every woman carries eggs from her grandmother and her mother. This means that in every woman alive at this moment, there is the embodied ancestral wisdom from two previous generations *as well as* the potential for the future. Not only do we have the disposition to walk and run toward the positive future that is possible, we have inherited wisdom to help guide our way.

As the author and mindfulness teacher Jack Kornfield writes, "The warrior in your heart says stand your ground. Feel the survival of a thousand years of ancestors in your muscles and your blood. You have all the support you need in your bones."

This Mother's Day, I am remembering my mother and grandmothers with gratitude. I am celebrating my children with presence. I am honoring the Earth Mother with love. Mothering is a devotional act. It is as hard, and as rewarding, as training for that marathon. I am leaning into the challenge. And I am going to start running again. There's a half marathon on a nearby wooded course in October, and I'll be there.

A Call to Action
Deepening

Generosity and Surrender

The peony blooms opened just days ago,
Soft round balls of warm pink
Sitting atop tall dark green stems.
The bulbs are clustered
But they open one at a time,
Each offering its fullness in turn.

Today, the large blossoms rest on the grass,
Heavy with their own weight
And the added weight of the rain that fell last night.

I wonder what twine or fencing I might have in
the barn.
I imagine I could create some support,
Alleviate the weight of their burden.

I watch an ant walk from a blade of grass
Into the heart of one of the blooms,
Disappearing into the soft sweet folds.

The ant is served by the weighted blossoms.
What else might benefit?
Maybe the drooping is part of the peony's offering,
A generous bowing to the earthbound insects
When it is done serving the airborne.
There is so much I do not know.

I am no longer wondering about twine and fencing.

I contemplate life and fullness,
Weight and burden, generosity and surrender,
Witnessing and honoring, beauty and decay.
The mysteries are infinite and close at hand.

Soft pink peony
Explosion of vibrant life
Rest your heavy head.

The beauty of the seasonal cycles, and my own learning, is that they are cyclical. As I have paid attention to them, I recognize how intimately connected they are. Noticing this, I am reminded, once again, that I am of this earth, a manifestation of the same creative impulse that is responsible for both the green and growing and the dead and dying around me. The shifting light and temperatures, the movement of the critters, and the activity or dormancy of the plant life are mirrored in the seasonally changing patterns in my own body, mind, and heart.

Each season of remembering carries me closer to my true nature. I also notice that there will be no arriving, only this movement onward. Like walking the labyrinth, there is only the turning, first inward and then outward and then inward again. This Great Turning—first to my heart and then to my family, my community, and the living Earth before turning in again—feels as natural and as critical as an exhale following an inhale. These patterns that repeat rather than resolve have a steadying, reassuring rhythm even as they nudge and push me into new corners of awareness and embrace of this life.

Interconnection

Householder Yoga

Upon ordination from the interfaith ministry program, I shared this vow with the congregation:

As I step into the wider community as an interfaith chaplain, I will lean into the divine, infinite, and eternal that is here, now, in this human, finite, and terrestrial life. Sacred One and Holy All.

During the service, as each ordinand shared a few words about how they would carry their work into the world, the rich diversity of human expression unfolded like a tapestry. At the center of the tapestry, our common divinity and humanity shone like the sun, offering light and life to this time of possibility.

Though ordination marks a closure, it also initiates a new beginning. A life of intention requires ongoing attention to the habits of heart and mind that connect or disconnect me from the world. I will continue to nurture the mindset, community, and practices that open me to the joy and the suffering in the world and allow me to meet them with compassion and love.

It is hard to answer the question that people often ask about my chaplaincy program: "What are you going to do with that?" Yesterday, it felt even more immediate when a few people asked,

"What are you going to do now?" Those are not easy questions to answer. For me, chaplaincy is more about "being" than it is about "doing." I know that doesn't translate easily in a culture that pays more attention to what we produce and consume than it does to how we engage. When I say "being," I mean a way of being fully present to myself, to the world, and to others.

My eyes and heart are open to the new opportunities that will inevitably emerge in the wider world now that I have passed through the threshold of ordination. For the summer, however, I will be sinking deeply into the spiritual practice of householder yoga, as described by the scholar and author Mirabai Starr in her book *Wild Mercy*: "If yoga means 'path to union with God,' then hooking up with a life partner and having kids together can be as valid—and certainly as rigorous—as living in an ashram engaged in spiritual discipline all day and into the night."

As I enter this new season of life as an interfaith minister, my children are entering the summer with new obligations, aspirations, and anticipations. The garden and the baby chickens require tending. Our household schedule and individual needs are all over the place, but the sense of safety and love in our home remains strong and consistent. This requires full attention and the intention to keep showing up to All That Is. The burnt toast, the laundry pile, the laughter, the weeds, the late nights, the cat barf on the stairs, the noise, the play, the frustration, the love. Sacred One and Holy All.

True Mother

Dropping Duncan off, I have the clear and distinct feeling that I am dropping him off to spend the month with his real mother. That's not to say that I am not the one who birthed him into this life. I was there for all nine months of gestation. I was there during the long prodromal labor and have been there for seventeen years of the joys and challenges that accompany growing up. It is always hard to say goodbye when we part ways, but then, it is never really hard. He is of the wide world and has always been eager to meet it. My job as a parent is, and always has been, to nurture, encourage, support, and let go. Letting go is the hardest part, but it is also something that I have an opportunity to practice quite regularly.

Today, as I leave him at the bottom of a trail in the Green Mountains, the letting go is eased by a sense of our shared belonging to something so much greater than ourselves. I remember with crystal clarity that he has a mother who is greater than me: this life-giving planet. If mother is the one who nourishes, protects, and teaches, introducing him to the mother of us all invites him into a wider sphere of protection and belonging than I, his human mother, can provide. As he widens his circle of care and attention in the world, it is so important for him to know that Mother Earth is always available to him. It matters for him, and it matters for the planet.

For a month, D will live under the wide sky with his hands in the earth and his heart to the land. He will sleep under stars and work in the rain, sun, heat, mud, and swarms of insects. The intellectual understanding that we are part of something larger will transform into a felt sense of belonging and participation. He will know that we are connected in biology and in spirit to the entire sphere of creation.

It is clear that our anthropocentric worldview has allowed humans to wreak havoc on the earth's systems. To interrupt our cycles of devastation, our relationships to each other and to the earth must change. Change will come more readily if we can move toward it with collective energy and intention. But to do that, we must know what we are moving toward. Fortunately, the living earth gives us that example in every system—collaborative, regenerative, sustainable. A natural system uses what it finds or manufactures in its proximity and recycles its "waste" back into utility. Humans could participate in and contribute to this holistic cycling. After all, we are creatures of this earth too. The same rules apply. But we have strayed far, and our culture keeps us from learning our true nature. We have become trapped in tight webs of human relationship instead of being able to expand into the web of the world community that includes the critters and plants, the breathing air, water, and soil. Our scurrying, rushing lifestyles have kept us from meeting and knowing our greater mother, yet she is still here.

She will hold, comfort, and teach us. We need only return to her to remember.

Gratitude Swells

A healthy ecosystem depends on many interconnected parts; logically, a healthy human system would as well. Despite the cultural myth that celebrates independence as a sign of optimal functioning, we are constantly giving and receiving throughout our lives. The risks we take by being vulnerable and open to the service of others are nothing compared to the risks we take by honoring individual independence above community. We rely on family, friends, neighbors, and strangers every day—and they are relying on us.

I often wonder how we can strengthen and honor our human connectivity. As the Fourth of July approached this year, I thought about building bridges, about traversing the distance and difference between independence and interdependence. With the help of a bit of wordplay, I demonstrated how you can get from one to the other with a few simple steps and how you can pause to dwell in any of the steps of the continuum. It went like this:

Independence
Separation, Autonomy
Rights, Responsibility, Integrity
Cooperation, Participation, Collaboration
Connection, Cohesion
Interdependence

I made it sound easy and tried to walk away as if it were a fait accompli. It wouldn't let me go. It's not that easy, and it's not the end of the process.

I was so eager to move beyond the discomfort of holding the contradictions of independence and interdependence in this time and place that I embraced the theoretical resolution of the wordplay. It did offer a sense of peace and completion for a spell and I was grateful for the breathing room. But the unease soon crept back in. Building bridges with words, ideas, and theories is only a starting point. The ideas that had originated in the head needed to land in the heart and be put into practice in the body. I am pulled to live into the pendulum of independence and interdependence in my own life. I need to pay attention to both the clinging and the releasing. I need to notice both the safety and the isolation, the comfort and the distress. I must actively choose to step in closer and invite others to join me in community. I must also pay attention when I am called to solitude.

Rather than building a bridge to span a gap, uniting my mind, body, and heart around these disparate ideas feels more like casting a wide net over abundance. It is about allowing and honoring the distance and potential between them. It is about knowing that those distances are full of potential and that, in that fertile space, there is infinite possibility and continual movement.

Today, rather than landing in something that looks like resolution, I am gaining comfort from the movement. I am appreciating my capacity to be elastic. Moving through my own ideas, embodied in emotions and actions, I live into the ebb and flow that guides all life. I inhale the sweet fragrance of the milkweed at the same moment the monarch lands to drink the flower's nectar. Gratitude swells as I walk on and the butterfly takes flight. Carrying the sweetness of the encounter for a moment longer, we go our separate ways, parting the same air that has sustained butterflies and humans for all time.

Gratitude and Responsibility

As the harvest season begins to slow, I am drawn toward incredible gratitude for the generous gifts of this life. What a gift it is to be here, now! We are invited to know and hold the horrors and traumas of our human past and present. We also get to be with the hard conversations, the healing, the wonder, the creativity. A walk through the garden, the forest, or along a city street puts it all on display. The dying and decay sit right next to the growth and possibility. My children help to keep me grounded in this balance. As representatives for all future generations, they remind me—and I am grateful for it—that there are others, and there will be others, for decades to come. This earth and this life are not mine to consume. They are only mine to tend and nurture. I am a custodian for present and future. I receive all that I have as a gift from those who came before, and I must steward it for all who will come after.

This responsibility, grounded in gratitude for the miracle of being here now, invigorates my personal values and motivates my work in the world. It is an aspirational and inspirational force. It helps that it is tidily packaged in the two bright-eyed young men whom I am grateful to call my sons. Their presence in our home and in our shared world is a daily reminder to be my best self.

I regularly feel this relationship between gratitude and responsibility in the garden. I am so grateful for the food that our garden produces and I feel responsible to the seedlings that we have planted. I feel a commitment to ensuring that they have ample sunlight and space for growing and producing. It is my responsibility to honor their potential by caretaking this space where they will live out their life cycle. I gratefully receive the gifts of the garden and offer it my labor in return. The reciprocity of this exchange feels right.

This summer, during a whirlwind visit of college campuses, Duncan and I attended a college president's address to prospective students and their guardians. This president lauded her school's dedication to its students and its deep commitment to fostering personal responsibility and accountability. As she spoke, it became clear how important this mission was to her. Then she segued into her own history. She described her father's experience of growing up watching his father work himself to exhaustion picking cotton. She described his resolve to ensure that his children would not pick cotton. She described what it meant to her that she was five generations away from slavery, a lawyer, the mother of triplets, and the president of a well-known college. In every facet of her story, she communicated her deep gratitude to the past and the awesome responsibility she felt to the present and the future.

Listening to her story, and her strength of conviction, I felt both my gratitude and my sense of responsibility rise—for her generously shared story and also for my own. We were about to interrupt our college visits with a vacation to the lake house that has been in our family for five generations. The parallels and contrasts in our stories demanded to be noticed. Not only that, they asked to be held gently, with awareness, and with gratitude and responsibility.

Faith

Peace at Sunset

Last night, as the sun was setting over the lake, the wind seemed to blow the thoughts from my mind as easily as it blew away the bugs and clouds. As my mundane and repetitive thoughts dissipated, my body grew calm and steady. The sky turned brilliant pinks and oranges, and a quiet peace returned to that place right beneath my breastbone where it lives much of the time. I hadn't even noticed it had been away. Welcoming that deep inner stillness home, I felt its presence permeate my body and spirit. I settled into it with a deep sigh.

That feels right.

Retracing the last days and weeks, I could not pinpoint the hour, or even the day, when my own grounding and inner stillness was replaced by the noisy chatter of contemporary life. But I could see why and how it had slipped beneath the surface. Over a series of days with more movement, more people, more obligations, and more schedules than usual, I was less attentive. Compelled to pay more attention to the needs and demands of the outer world, I let the care and nourishment of my inner world wane. For most of the summer, I had been paying very careful attention to balancing the needs of my spirit with the needs of the world. And now I hadn't even noticed that I had slipped.

I only needed the sunset to bring me back to myself.

Dwelling in the balance between inner and outer, giving and receiving, doing and resting seems to be at the center of the householder yoga that I have been practicing this summer. While life requires us to navigate the practical needs and emotions along the entire arc of a swinging pendulum, the perpetual movement invites us to remain confident that we will always return to center. Even the highest tide will ebb. The setting sun suggests that a sunrise is on the way.

Just after the sun rose this morning, I paddled across the lake. I gave thanks as I fell deep into that inner stillness still swelling beneath my breastbone. I am grateful for the remembering ushered in by last night's breezy sunset and for the pendulum that carries me reliably between the work of sustaining my spirit and the work of sustaining my family and community. These two things are not just related, they are aspects of a singular ongoing movement. In *A Gift from the Sea*, Anne Morrow Lindbergh describes the movement this way: "The only continuity possible, in life as in love, is in growth, in fluidity—in freedom, in the sense that the dancers are free, barely touching as they pass, but partners in the same pattern."

Roots and Rocks

On a well-worn trail, roots and rocks seem to rise above the surface at unpredictable intervals and angles. They have been exposed by the compaction of soil caused by footfall and water. With human travelers kept to one narrow pathway, impact is consolidated into the sacrifice zone that is the trail.

This sacrificial zone is both a challenge and a benefit to the trees and bushes that grow in close proximity to the trail. The trail corridor reduces canopy competition, giving each individual plant increased access to sunlight. However, the roots that get exposed by the trail bed have to work harder to extract water from the compacted soil. They are also more vulnerable to insects, hooves, and Vibram soles of passersby.

The runners and walkers who travel the trail also have a challenge and an opportunity. A single moment of inattention or distraction can send a person rolling downhill when a toe gets caught on a rock or root. As reminders to stay aware and attentive, these obstacles become opportunities. They provide a chance to concentrate thoroughly on each moment, movement, and part of the trail. For today, this rocky, rooty obstacle course is my mindfulness training.

But it's not really the ground directly underneath my feet that matters. Even as I take a step, I need to be anticipating the next one. At a stroll, I can safely look a dozen meters ahead, scanning back to the near ground with each new step. At a slow run, I can look only two meters ahead or less. It seems a fitting metaphor for the way I move through life. When I am moving along at a clip, I can attend only to that which is immediately in front of me. If I am not careful, I am liable to be surprised when I suddenly notice changes in terrain, scenery, or company along the trail. I remain alert and acutely present to the near ground. When I am walking the trail at a more leisurely pace, I have a little wider perspective. I am inclined to develop expectations and anticipation based on what I have glimpsed up the trail, but I am in no hurry to arrive there. I am content in each step. As I relax into the place and my pace, time and thought dissolve and I feel myself melt into the forest landscape.

The hustle and the saunter are neither good nor bad. I am not making a judgment, just noticing that they are different, and require different responses from me. At either pace, the only way forward is one careful step at a time.

At the Woodpile

There have been many years when I have found myself living with a general malaise when the days begin to get shorter and colder. My energy wanes and doubt and uncertainty creep in.

How much snow will there be? Will the roof get ice dams? How cold will it get? Will there be enough wood? Should we get more? How will we pay for it?

These nagging questions about myriad unknowns tend to throw me into a cycle of anxiety and fear. I begin to feel tension in my shoulders. They rise up toward my ears—not just hunched as if to ward off cold, but hunched as if to ward off life.

This year feels different. As the dark season approaches, I remain curious and open. I am attentive to the fact that this ebb in the tide of the year is critical to the overall balance. The cold and darkness are necessary counters to the heat and light, just as the exhale is as critical as the inhale. Just as the trees seem to sigh with relief as they release their leaves, I am eager to let go and let be in this season.

Not content to just appreciate this change of heart, I begin to wonder where it came from. The answer that emerges surprises me. *Faith.*

I had never thought of myself as a person of faith. I had always understood faith as a very simple, but also very complete, belief and confidence in God. Wrapped up in this definition was an understanding of a God that was external, distant, and defined by doctrine. I couldn't really relate to that God, much less have faith in Him (or Her). The god of my experience is close—in my heart, in the sun that rises each morning and sets each evening. It's in the moon and stars that govern the night whether we see them or not. The god of my experience is the light that flows through each one of us and permeates everything around us. The god of my experience sends love notes in the form of dreams, birds, people, and water droplets that catch the sun—and so much more. The god of my experience is the divine, the Unknowable Mystery, the

Universal Spirit, the Source, love, light, joy … and oak, rock, moss, earthworm, eagle, salmon, child, stream, ocean, moon, sun.

I haven't been able to name and claim the divine of my own experience for very long. But apparently it's been long enough for the seed of knowing to grow into faith.

Nurturing this nascent faith involves paying attention to the natural world around me, noticing the beauty in all things, including (and maybe especially) that which is tragic and heartbreaking. There is divine expression in decay as well as in creation; the interplay between them is constant. Since recognizing that all the world is divine expression, my attention to the embodiment of spirit in the natural environment has been heightened. In witness to cycles of emergence, life, and decay in the garden, field, and forest, I more fully recognize my own participation in the cycle as well. Accepting this without reluctance or embrace is a practice of letting go and letting be.

Play of Dark and Light

Since the fall equinox, the periods of darkness in each day have gotten longer. By Samhain, at the end of October, we had entered the darkest stretch of the year, with darkness growing each day. Until the winter solstice on December 21, the amount of light that shines on our hemisphere will continue to decrease. My body responds to the darkness in a few ways. I sleep longer. I crave warm, heavy, sweet foods. I get crabby and weepy more often. The double whammy of dark and cold saps my motivation for exercise and social engagement. Maintaining either requires discipline and intention—both of which seem to require an inordinate amount of energy to summon.

But there's another aspect to the darkness, too, where a certain spaciousness and timelessness creep in and a different capacity is opened. I chop piles of vegetables to make big pots of healthy, hearty soups and stews. I sit by the fire for long periods and read or write or knit or sit in contemplation. Those long nights of sleep invite interesting, thought-provoking dreams. When I wake, the night lingers in my semiconscious mind as I slowly stretch. With night fading and day dawning, I know that god is here in the darkness, too. The dark calls me inward toward the divine within me.

I have been thinking about the imagery of light. Many faith traditions express the divine as light, and in Quaker tradition, we speak often of the light—as in "I am holding you in the Light" and "the Light of God is within each one of us." This imagery of divine light is evocative. With this word, *light*, we are able to name the unnameable, to contain the essence of the Unknowable Mystery in a word that we can hold in our hearts, tend with our sacred imaginations, honor with our prayers and actions, and name when it washes over and through us. The Light pulls me into the open and seems to invite clear seeing. The Light calls me outward to the divine that illuminates all.

It feels important to point out that our culture has distorted the concepts of light and dark in devastating ways. The value judgments that have been assigned to light and dark have had profound negative impacts on our relationships with ourselves, with one another, and with the earth. As an amateur naturalist and a writer, however, I am compelled to reclaim the words and the powerful imagery they carry. My desire to name and embrace the light and the dark nudges me more deeply into the indescribable fullness of the divine existence that I witness and live within every day.

Consider the balance and resonance of light and dark by approaching each of these questions as a meditation.

What does it mean that the Light of God is within you?

Is the light a candle that flickers and dims according to the amount of air that it is offered?

How do you carry it?

Is your light more like a campfire?

Do you feed it slowly and steadily with branches of courage, hope, resolve, and rest?

Does the fire ever dwindle to a pile of embers?

How do you greet the darkness?

Is it a cocoon—a place of transformation and safety apart from the world?

Is the darkness like a cave, a place of respite during a storm or the heat of the midday?

Or is it a place to be avoided, full of unknown dangers?

Is the darkness a void, absent of time, space, light, and being?

I suspect that I am not alone in having more positive responses to images and ideas of light. We tend to avoid that which we cannot see, understand, or appreciate. We pursue the seen, the known, and the familiar. But this season is an opportunity to befriend the darkness and embrace the beauty and the mystery that dwell there. If you are an early riser, resist the urge to turn on the lights when you first wake. For a few minutes—or a few hours—allow your pace to match the pace of the waking earth. Notice the way the darkness recedes to the gathering light. If you are a night owl, turn off the lights a few hours before you go to sleep. Become familiar with the shape and shadows of your house in moonlight and starlight. Your pace will slow to help protect you from bumping into walls. As it does, notice the still and guiding presence within you and surrounding you.

In the season of darkness, let us hold our friends in the light. Let us also sit with them in the dark. Give thanks to the Unknowable Mystery.

Grace

In Community

I amble across the field, a single human moving through a quiet morning. I am heading away from the road, away from the farmhouse, and away from the ducks floating on the pond. I am heading toward an expanse of grass that leads to a marshy waterway. But mostly I am not heading anywhere. I am just meandering through the field, aware of everything and nothing at the same time. Until my field of vision shifts.

The grassy hillside ahead of me seems to glisten in the hazy light. Looking closer, to the ground at my feet, I notice that a drop of rain is suspended on each branch of each blade of grass. I stoop to appreciate one particular plant and the drops that have gathered on its tips and notches. Here, in singular form, each drop rests in intimate relationship with the part of the plant on which it landed. By nearly impossible odds, that particular drop landed on that particular crevice of this particular plant. And now it rests in such comfort and union that, to my outsider's view, the plant and raindrop appear to have always been in relation to one another. The drop will remain where it is until it is released by a passing critter, evaporated by warmth and sun, dried by the wind, or swept away by another raindrop falling to the earth. The drop is singular, and also a part of a whole. The one in the all and the all in the one. Each drop came from a body of water and each drop will return to another body of water eventually. It separates, returns to a source, and separates again, the water cycle mirroring the life cycle.

Later in my walk, I startle a lone turkey and then a deer, each of us ambling in solitude until, of course, we notice one another. Then we are in community with each other. And, in community, we are one. Each of us—water droplet, human, turkey, deer—is one of many. And we are each part of a singular whole, held in the grace of this particular time and place.

In this space, there are no more words. There is only awe, gratitude, and responsibility to this oneness. This is grace. Rest here with me for a few moments.

Footprints on the Beach

Walking on the beach, I am aware that the track of footprints I am leaving behind me gives the illusion that I am here alone. In fact, though my body is unaccompanied today, my heart has company. Above there is a big, wide sky, and each time I look up to it, I can hear my dad's familiar exclamation: "Blue, blue, blue!" This is the kind of sky that fills the chest, expanding it with warmth despite the cold. This is the kind of sky that we used to gaze into seemingly endlessly as we walked the beach, wordless except for the spoken appreciation for all that blue.

Three gulls stand at the water's edge, their feathers puffed out for warmth. Their lack of movement on this chilly morning tells me that they are holding court here, attending, greeting, and witnessing. I follow their gaze to the ocean and find myself drawn to that place just beyond the horizon. It is that place, just out of sight, that calls me. I long for it, gaze after it, and even walk toward it, right up to the water's edge. Mingled with my longing for that which is beyond the horizon, that which is inaccessible, is my appreciation. There is so much that lies beyond my seeing and beyond my knowing. With my toes licked by the incoming waves, I turn to retrace my steps. Longing reaches out to hold hands with wonder and I follow them down the beach.

I follow my footprints back to the trail that leads away from the beach. It is not my day to drift into the mystery; it is my time for communion with all that I can see—this blue sky, these plump gulls, my solitary footprints along the beach. Blessedly, there is also communion with much that I cannot see, a palpable love and oneness that emerge as memories from the sand with each soft footfall. As I walk through the softball- and baseball-sized rocks that separate the beach and the trail, I have a sense that I am walking back toward the seen, into the realm of the knowable, the striving, and the pretending to know. Leaving the limitless expanse of the beach and returning to the confines of a trail, I fall back into my body.

The pampas grass along the estuary waves playfully while a songbird chirps incessantly from somewhere just beyond my sight. "Not so fast," he seems to say. "There is always more than meets the eye." The past and the future are always walking with me. Love and light extend beyond boundaries of time, space, and physical body. The creative universe is infinite and ever expanding *and* it is all available, always. There are simply some places where I can access that knowing more readily. Or perhaps these are the places where that knowing can access me. Either way, when I am longing for a visit to the beach, I know that I am really longing for a reconnection to All That Is.

Persistence

I doubt that I can pull it off. I give it too much weight and myself not enough courage, or skill, or endurance. None of that, of course, is true. I am enough. Furthermore, I am not doing it alone. I am never alone. The Universal Spirit of all life is within me and all around me. That is enough, certainly. And the gods and goddesses of creativity midwife all creative acts. I am sure that I do not ever write from myself alone. There are always muses in my fingertips and in my heart, making words into art.

I look to the birch tree leafing out in the sunroom. We cut it from the forest to be a Christmas tree and "planted" it in a pot of rocks and water, hopeful that it would sprout roots and we would be able to replant it when the ground thaws in a few more months. Now, with tender buds opening into leaves, the birch tree is a reminder of life's persistence and the eventuality of emergence. It reminds me to stay the course, to trust the process. It reminds me to put down roots and risk leafing out. Both are needed. The steady foundation of roots balances the expansion of the spring-green leaves. The birch tree emanates patience and faith.

Those two qualities continue to arise for me these days. They are interrelated, it seems. Faith allows for patience to take hold, and patience is required to cultivate an abiding faith. Persistence marries them—the persistence of the will to let go and the persistence of the commitment to divine presence. The divine insists that I live into the possibilities of my life. The divine insists that I use my inclination for observation and words to guide others toward their own observations and intentions. The divine insists on life, revealed always through our hearts and our hands, our heads and our homes, the hearths where we nurture and grow the stories of our lives. How these elements mingle for me is intriguing.

I am not sure that they even separate well. They certainly interweave in some sort of beautiful Celtic knot. My heart aches to comfort the hurting world around me. My hands move to offer work in service. My head seeks to observe, understand, and connect. The hearth of my home sustains me, nourishing my inner and outer being. It is also a means of providing comfort to others, a place to use my hands and heart in service. The heart signifies the calling at the center of my being. I extend myself outward through my head, hands, and hearth. Yes, I can see the image: the heart in the center, the hands extending to the side, the head extending upward, and the hearth at my feet, grounding me in this place, these people, and this time.

These reflections from the hearth and trail are the story of the trail I follow, the one that always leads back to the ground beneath my feet. Sometimes you must travel far to find what is near. The trails of my life extend out from the hearth and return always to the hearth, a path of knowing that follows the heart outward and ever homeward. The hearth and the trail weave together in ever-repeating, ever-returning patterns. There is beauty in the repetition, and there is balance in the departures and the returns.

Equilibrium

This morning, long shadows stretch out across the new snow. I look up to see the waning moon shining bright, and the contrasts are dazzling. The bright moon hangs in the fading night sky, a brilliant beacon portaging awe. The crisp, lean lines of the tree shadows lie on the ground, a study in boundaries and steady presence.

This morning's play between darkness and light is a relief. The strong contrasts are beautiful. Though sharp, the edges feel almost soft. In these illuminated differences, there is truth and integrity. It is a relief to know, if only for these few moments of early morning, that there is beauty in the place where the light and the dark meet. I immediately recognize the relevant lesson for my life. Rather than becoming exhausted or overstretched by trying to embrace the immensity of contrasting strong emotions, I can relax into the place where they meet, noticing tension and contrast and also beauty. This simple noticing takes me off the roller coaster in my head and heart and onto my feet, rooted firmly in this generous earth. My attention turns fully to the mundane tasks in front of me, easing me gently into the day as I make breakfast, fill the woodstove, and pack lunch boxes.

An hour later, the night shadows have given way to a ubiquitous softness. As the winter sunrise casts its pale light across the sky and snowy landscape, everything is washed in gauze, including my newfound clarity. I am suddenly washed in gauze too. What am I doing now? Can it be done faster so I can move on to something else? What happened to that sense of peace? It was just here. I could feel it. And now it has slipped away.

My moment of frustration and disappointment gives way to a laugh. After all, this is the way of the world. Why should it be any different for me? There is coalescing and there is dispersal. There is coming together and there is resting apart. There are phases and stages. I can only endeavor to pay attention and to learn from each step along the way. I do not need to ride the roller coaster, but I can pay attention to the ups and downs. I can remember that the moon and the long lines of the tree shadows teach. So does the soft, gauze-washed sky. And I can remember to hold and release it all lightly.

May you, too, notice the teachings that arrive unbidden in your day.

May you hold them with love, levity, and generosity.

May you release them with love, levity, and generosity.

Emergence

Morning Light

I enjoy the darkness of the early morning. It has a nurturing softness. In the still-dark house, I move slowly and intentionally through my morning routine. Before too much movement or thought shakes the dreamy sleep from my head, I turn on the coffee pot and roll out my yoga mat in the living room for twenty minutes of gentle yoga and stretching. This quiet, prayerful moving meditation invites my breath to slowly and gently waken my muscles and my mind. In the still-dark morning, the monkey mind is still sleeping and the demands of the day have not yet arrived. I am not only surrounded by silence and stillness, but filled with it as I fill my lungs with each breath. I set my intentions for the day during this quiet interlude between night and day, sleep and wakefulness.

With a bow to the rising sun that is still not yet peeking over the horizon, I roll up my mat and move to the kitchen. The coffee is ready. As I pour a cup, I notice the light coming from the chicken coop. I can only smile as I stand in my dark, quiet kitchen looking through the dark, still yard to that beam of light. The coop is probably bright and noisy as the hens and rooster shake off the night in their own way. They will be stretching their wings, chattering and mingling about. I wonder if they are noticing that one of their friends spent the night outside. (We couldn't find her when we closed up last night.) I will let the chickens out to explore the yard after it has gotten a little lighter. The rooster will crow to let me know when it is time.

Still moving gently through the dark, I take a shower and get dressed. Coming out of the bathroom, I hear Thatcher stirring upstairs, heading to his shower. That is my cue that the day is arriving. It is time for me to move out of this dreamy transition zone and into the morning too. This time, I turn on the light as I enter the kitchen to make breakfast and pack lunches. By the time I am done, there will be enough light outside to take Karma for a walk and let the chickens out of the coop so they can spend the day grazing. The day has arrived, and I am ready to step gladly into the light.

Throughout the day, I will touch back into the morning's stillness that is stored in the muscle memory of my body, mind, and heart. It remains closer and clearer on some days more than others. I appreciate it when it is close, but the outcome is not the point. I just get to tend the practice with care and love each morning and strive to cultivate the same degree of intentionality throughout the day. And I get to share it all with you. May my morning reflection invite you to pause and embrace the dark and light of your own rising day.

Unfolding

On Thursday evening, I finally noticed that I had been burning my candle at both ends. I had hit the proverbial wall. When an event that I had been planning to attend on Saturday was canceled, I made a commitment to recalibrate. As I crossed the item off my calendar, I noticed that I could, with just a little more schedule wiggling, claim seventy-two hours of rest time. Rest is not easy for me. I tend to use extra minutes in my day to catch up on a project here or fit in a little correspondence there. But my intention was to find ease, to put some distance between my body, my mind, and the insistence to be productive. I would attempt to practice non-productivity. Over those seventy-two hours, I did not set my morning alarm or follow my regular morning routines. I did not insist on anything except for being non-productive. As I observed, relaxed, and found stillness, I regained some balance. I emerged feeling rested.

Over those same seventy-two hours, our community began to respond to the coronavirus pandemic in amazing and beautiful ways. Individuals, organizations, schools, and businesses are prioritizing community health and safety over any other agenda. People are choosing to stay home, grounding themselves in order to provide a measure of distance and protection to unknown individuals. I have never seen this kind of compassionate selflessness on this scale in my lifetime. I am falling in love with humanity anew. Business as usual has been interrupted in a most extraordinary way.

There are disappointments, inconveniences, and real hardships involved in this interruption. The impact will not be evenly distributed across our population. Those who are most vulnerable because of age, illness, or access to resources will be hit the hardest by the virus and our country's response to it. It is not fair. If I stop there, I am swallowed by the shame, sadness, and anger that arise with this awareness. If I continue, it is hard not to notice that this also feels like an incredible opportunity.

Yes, there is injustice. Yes, there is fear. Yes, there is even death. We will all be touched by deep, heart-opening loss. But there is also great love in our collective response. I am encouraged by that. I am praying that we use this time to recalibrate, to accelerate our movement toward a world that is more just, more sustainable, more aligned with our true nature. I do not have any answers, but I am sitting with openness, curiosity, and a strong belief in our capacity for change. Hope lives here. I offer some of it to you:

As we slow down and encounter our fears, worries, and regrets,
> *What peace will we find in the spaciousness of our newly collapsed schedules?*
> *What love is holding us aloft?*
> *What belonging is soothing our isolation?*

As we spend more time in our homes and local communities,
> *What bridges will we build?*
> *What support will we offer to others?*
> *What support will we need from others?*

As we notice the impacts of our lives on the lives of others,
> *Will we claim our participation in the web of life?*
> *Will we remember the legacy of survival that ensured our lives?*
> *Will we remember that we will one day be the ancestors in someone else's story?*

As we recognize our depth of responsibility to the interconnected human family,
> *Will we also notice our interconnection with all living beings?*
> *Will we notice our interconnection with the living, pulsing earth?*
> *Will we notice that we are, in fact, One?*

The lily and tulip spears nudging through the barely thawed soil in my yard are a prelude to the new season. May we also enter this season as neophytes, open to the promise and surprise of our own unfolding.

May we be well. May we be safe. May we be healthy. May we be at peace.

Getting to Work

The blazing orange sun is low on the horizon when it catches my eye, as well as my heart and imagination. Like a candle that has been touched gently by a match, I spring to life, a flurry of activity and energy. Not sure where to put it, I clean the house, literally. I know where this energy is intended to go. I am supposed to be writing this morning. But there is something to clear before I can settle in front of the keyboard. My writing emerges from my lived experience, but it also meets with the wider world in some universal expression. As I dust and declutter, I am not "gathering my thoughts." I am creating space for thoughts and feelings to arrive from beyond me. I am making space for wonder, inspiration, and ideation. I am readying myself. Readying for whatever this creative spark of inspiration will become. Readying for whatever fire kindles to life within me. Readying to allow my own flaming energy to expand and rise to meet the flaming sun.

The sun and I are two kindred spirits offering light and heat. In fact, we are all kindred spirits, balls of potential linked by a thread. Perhaps it is really a wick that runs between us. Once ignited, we need only to allow the energy to flow through us. We need to stop cleaning the house and sit down at the keyboard. Rather, *I* need to stop cleaning the house, and *I* need to sit down at the keyboard. I am very familiar with my methods of procrastination. They need to be acknowledged, but I also need to be careful not to indulge them or fall too deeply into their grip.

I am meant to live in this time and place deeply, to notice, reflect, and share. This sharing is the work I am meant to offer. Gathering my thoughts, feelings, and questions into words to share in blog posts, books, and poems is one way that I can cast heat and light back out into the world. I am grateful for the gifts of my life and I feel responsible for passing them on. In her essay "Of Power and Time," the poet Mary Oliver cautions, "The most regretful people on earth are those who felt the call to creative work, who felt their own creative power restive and uprising, and gave to it neither power nor time." I intend not to be regretful. I will give both power and time to my creative work. To do that, I have to remind myself to value it. I have to remind myself that it is the work I am here to do. And sometimes I need to procrastinate a little bit before getting to it.

I believe that each one of us has a role to play in the continually unfolding story of the universe.

Do you know what your role is?

Do you know what you need to do to allow your creative energy to burst forth?

Is there something you need to stop doing?

Is there something you need to start doing?

Those are big questions. Maybe they sound like more pressure and more expectation coming at you from the outside world. But they are not questions that need answers. I simply invite you to sit with them from time to time.

Today, if you can, sit with them in the warmth of the sun for a few minutes. Allow yourself to be open to possibility. Allow yourself to be warmed and nourished. Allow yourself to notice the heat that is within you meeting the heat that is outside of you. Trust that you know how and when to offer your heat and light to the world around you.

When you return to your day, may you return with a little extra light. And may that light kindle a flame in someone else, who kindles a flame in someone else, who kindles …

Consider the Raindrop

Consider the raindrop,
    falling to earth, singular and newly formed,
        carrying millennia of history, information, and
            form in its molecules.

Consider the raindrop,
    nourishing soil, growing plants and animals,
        creating, feeding, and cleansing all life.

Consider the raindrop,
    tumbling into cracks and crevices,
        following millions of raindrops through
            unmarked paths carved into the landscape
            over centuries.

Consider the raindrop,
    giving itself in communion with a trickle before
        tumbling into a river that
            rolls into an estuary and
            commingles with the ocean.

Consider the raindrop,
    entering your body
        as water, food, creation, or inspiration,
            filling you with life and possibility.

Consider the *thousands* of raindrops that are in *you*.

Further Reading

Mystic Journey: Getting to the Heart of Your Soul's Story,
Robert Atkinson

The Story of Our Time: From Duality to Interconnectedness to Oneness, Robert Atkinson

The Gift of Stories: Practical and Spiritual Applications of Autobiography, Life Stories, and Personal Mythmaking,
Robert Atkinson

Visit robertatkinson.net for more information about personal mythmaking.

If Women Rose Rooted: A Life-Changing Journey to Authenticity and Belonging, Sharon Blackie

Callings: Finding and Following an Authentic Life, Gregg Levoy

Active Hope: How to Face the Mess We're in without Going Crazy,
Joanna Macy and Chris Johnstone

Conversation—The Sacred Art: Practicing Presence in an Age of Distraction, Diane M. Millis, PhD

Sacred Instructions: Indigenous Wisdom for Living Spirit-Based Change, Sherri Mitchell

A Hidden Wholeness: The Journey Toward an Undivided Life,
Parker J. Palmer

On the Brink of Everything: Grace, Gravity, and Getting Old,
Parker J. Palmer

Soulcraft: Crossing into the Mysteries of Nature and Psyche,
Bill Plotkin

Wild Mercy: Living the Fierce and Tender Wisdom of the Women Mystics, Mirabai Starr

The Mystic Heart: Discovering a Universal Spirituality in the World's Religions, Wayne Teasdale

The Book of Joy, His Holiness the Dalai Lama and Archbishop Desmond Tutu, with Douglas Abrams

About the Author

In her actions and her words, Lisa Steele-Maley weaves together her roles as mother, daughter, wife, writer, and educator. Ordained by the Chaplaincy Institute of Maine (ChIME) in 2019, Lisa is an interfaith minister who nurtures the fierce and tender connections between self, spirit, land, and community. Her writing reflects a strong connection to the affirming rhythms of the natural world and keen attention to the details of daily living and relationships.

Her first book, *Without a Map: A Caregiver's Journey through the Wilderness of Heart and Mind,* was published in 2018. Since then, she has regularly shared reflections at lisa.steelemaley.io. Lisa lives in an aging farmhouse on the coast of Maine with her husband, two teenage sons, and a handful of animals.

Praise for
*Without a Map: A Caregiver's Journey
through the Wilderness of Heart and Mind*

Without a Map *measures up to my sense of what makes a book not just good but superb. In Lisa Steele-Maley's graceful prose—which is a joy to read—you see a fine mind and a loving heart at work. Her use of her frequent forays into the wilderness as a metaphor for her journey with her beloved father thru the thickets of Alzheimer's disease gave me more guidance than I received from learning science-based "tips, tricks, and techniques" as I tried to accompany my mother on the same journey.... I finished the book with a more understanding heart, more courage (at age 80) to face into my own old age, and with a smile on my face: While it's true that there is no map for the perplexing journey with a loved one lost in Alzheimer's disease, Lisa Steele-Maley in this beautiful book has provided us with a metaphorical map that I found profoundly inspiring and useful. I believe that you will, too.*

—Parker J. Palmer, author of *On the Brink of Everything*
and *Let Your Life Speak*

This book is an exquisite, personal account of the journey of the author becoming caregiver for her father during his experience with dementia. There are innumerable people who would appreciate the wisdom in this book: people living with or near progressive terminal disease, caregivers, healthcare providers, contemplative seekers, attuned parents, and conscious human beings. The pace is perfect, the structure balanced, the length just-right, and the message is one that transcends this family and this diagnosis. For anyone who seeks peace and growth from within life's most trying, potentially most distressing, and ultimately most life-affirming places, this book will bring you near that beautiful, terrible edge.... Take it in and it will leave a mark on you.

—Dr. Sarah Rossmassler, Palliative Care Nurse Practitioner

In Without a Map *Lisa Steele-Maley invites us to pause, embrace our loved ones, and embrace the good that is in each moment as we come to accept the unknown together. Steele-Maley offers solidarity and hope, along with many examples of practical problem-solving, to anyone who is in a position to care for an aging parent or loved one. Her own walk with her father through the profoundly destabilizing experience of his illness and passing is recounted honestly, but Steele-Maley reminds us that caregiving can open us up to awe and reverence for the wonder that each life really is.*

—Elizabeth Gibbons Capdevielle, PhD,
University Writing Program, University of Notre Dame